# PREFACE

This bibliography provides annotations on future trends in terrorism from open-source literature published between 1996 and mid-1998. The dominant trend discussed in this literature is the increasing likelihood that terrorists will use weapons of mass destruction (WMD), particularly against the United States. Accordingly, many of the 295 monographs and journal articles surveyed in this bibliography discuss the potential threats of nuclear, biological, and chemical terrorism and the countermeasures that need to be implemented in responding to these threats. A number of other articles discuss the emerging threat of computer or cyberterrorism and the potential threat to the United States' information-technology (IT)-based infrastructure. Many articles discuss new technologies to counter more conventional terrorist threat, such as detecting bombs at airports.

The compilers of the bibliography have endeavored to include the most recent, relevant, and substantive articles on terrorism (those published in 1998) from journals, news magazines, selected newspapers, and monographs. The bibliography also includes relevant items published in 1996–97 but not annotated for the Federal Research Division's previous terrorism bibliographies (June 1993 and October 1997). Several foreign-language items have been includes and are indicated as such. In general, however, the effort focused on English-language sources.

The bibliography is organized into six geographic regions—Africa, Asia, Europe, Latin American, the Middle East, and North America—as well as a general International section. Most entries are listed under the International and North America sections. All entries have keywords, such as antiterrorism, WMD, cyberterrorism, and others. Upon request, the Federal Research Division will supply specialized, subject-oriented or geographical printouts.

# TABLE OF CONTENTS

**Africa**

Anonymous. "International: A Case of Mistaken Identity?," Economist, 348, No. 8083, August 29, 1998, 43-44.

The cruise missile attack on Sudan by the United States has aroused general skepticism, but the Sudanese government, which has alienated many of its neighbors, is finding that it has few friends, above all powerful friends, who are willing to come openly to its defense. After cruise missiles destroyed the Shifa pharmaceuticals factory in Khartoum on August 20, Sudan invited the United Nations to search the site for traces of the chemical-weapons components that, according to the United States, were the reason for the strike. The UN Security Council prevaricated, and the region has not rallied behind Sudan.

Keyword(s): combating terrorism; counterterrorism; CBRNC; chemical weapons of mass destruction

Anonymous. "Bombings Reiterate Need to Protect Windows," Security, 35, No. 9, September 1998, 109. The two bombings of U.S. embassies in Kenya and Tanzania in August 1998 are the latest tragedies to demonstrate the devastation that the combination of bombs and window glass can cause. In an interview, Rob Martin, director of the Technical Advisory Committee on Blast Resistant Glazing Systems, discussed the use of security and safety window film as a means of reducing death, injury, and property damage.

Keyword(s): antiterrorism; combating terrorism; infrastructure protection; technology; blast mitigation

Block, Robert. "Kenya, Tanzania Offer Fertile Soil for Intrigue," Wall Street Journal, August 11, 1998, A12.

The search for an answer to the causes of the recent bombings of two US embassies in East Africa may relate to economic and security conditions in Kenya and Tanzania. Both are poverty-ridden countries in which bribery and money-making schemes are common and law-enforcement and security lax. In the case of Kenya, the country has recently experienced outbreaks of state-sponsored violence, destroying respect for the state, its institutions, and its laws. A proliferation of weapons, porous borders, and rampant government corruption are factors that may have proven attractive to terrorists wishing to strike at the United States via its embassies in vulnerable capitals. lb

Keyword(s): terrorism; terrorist groups and activities; future trends

"Gangsters Against Gangsterism"s," Foreign Report,[Surrey], no. 2520, November 12, 1998, 1-2.

Security officials in South Africa have reported the existence of a terrorist organization based in Cape Town. Known as "People Against Gangsterism and Drugs" (Pagan), South African police believe the group has received training in Iran, Libya, and Sudan and may have been responsible for one or more terrorist bombings in South Africa. The Iranian government has denied having links with Pagan, but authorities note a virulent anti-Americanism among some Muslims in South Africa that may have Iranian

1

roots.

Keyword(s): terrorist groups and activities; terrorism


Gunby, Phil. "US Military Medicine Responds to Results of Terrorism in Africa," JAMA [Journal of the American Medical Association], 280, No. 10, September 9, 1998, 870-71.

The bombings of the U.S. embassies in Kenya and Tanzania on August 7, 1998, have proven once again the importance of high-speed, flexible medical response. U.S. Air Force, Air National Guard, and Air Force Reserve medical people flew approximately 4,000 miles from Germany to provide care within 20 hours of the explosions that killed 250 people and wounded 5,000 others. Twenty-two patients, all in critical condition, were flown from Nairobi to Ramstein, and eight of these patients were subsequently flown by the U.S. Air Force to the military's Walter Reed Medical Center in Washington, D.C. Other medical assistance is also discussed.

Keyword(s): terrorism (general); antiterrorism; first responders; combating terrorism


McKinley, James C. Jr. "Security Flaws Left Embassy in Nairobi Open to Attack," New York Times, September 9, 1998, A6.

The American Embassy in Nairobi was an easy target for terrorists. Its perimeter was patrolled by unarmed guards earning about $100 a month. The embassy's parking lot, shared with a bank, had an exit lane protected by neither guards nor barricades. On August 7, 1998, attackers in a truck packed with explosives turned off Haile Selassie Avenue and roared up that lane, flashing past an uninstalled security barrier that the bank was planning to erect to protect the lot. The truck managed to drive close to the building, where it was stopped by an unarmed private security guard at a barrier at the entrance to an underground garage. The guard ran when the attackers threw a grenade-like device at him.

Keyword(s): antiterrorism; combating terrorism; counterterrorism


Pereira, Paul. "SA's Weimar Inheritance," Finance Week, 76, No. 35, September 3-9, 1998, 68-69.

An old phenomenon, terrorism began with the kamikaze-style raids of the Islamic Sunni assassinations of Christians in the Crusader Kingdom of the twelfth century. Although the liberation of the communist states has ended terrorism in countries such as Germany, Italy, and Japan, terrorism continues apace in the Middle East and to a lesser extent in Northern Ireland. As a political strategy, terrorism has often failed. Yet Africa's flirtation with terrorism has had results.

Keyword(s): terrorist groups and activities; future trends; terrorism

Venter, Al J. "Targeting Sudan: Why We Bombed Osama bin Laden's Shadowy World of Intrigue," Soldier of Fortune, 23, No. 12, December 1998, 48-51, 69.

The author suggests that the U.S. bombing of Khartoum's Al Shifa Pharmaceutical factory was probably a mistake. Nevertheless, he describes as "irrefutable" that the soil sample clandestinely removed from the factory's rose garden "does present incontrovertible evidence of EMPTA...," a precursor for the deadly manufacture of VX nerve gas. The article discusses Osama bin Laden and Sudan's status as a pariah state as well as a puppet state of Iran.

Keyword(s): counterterrorism; combating terrorism; terrorism; terrorist groups and activities

Weiser, Benjamin. "A Ben Laden Agent Left Angry Record of Gripes and Fears," New York Times, December 12, 1998, A1 and A6.

Weiser discusses information gleaned from a computer seized in Nairobi, Kenya, following the embassy bombing in August 1998. One message in particular offers insight into the Ben Laden terrorist network's organization and operations in East Africa prior to the bombing, including the use of CNN and the Internet. The writer was Haroun Fazil, one of the prime suspects in the bombing. [lb]

Keyword(s): terrorist groups and activities; counterterrorism

## Asia

Anonymous. "'Copycat' Terrorism in Japan," <u>Japan Times Weekly</u> <u>International Edition</u>, 38, No. 38, September 21-27, 1998, 20.

An editorial addresses a series of mysterious poisoning cases that has sent a shock wave across Japan in recent months. The latest incidents happened on September 7, 1998, when two men fell ill after drinking coffee.

Keyword(s): terrorist cults; terrorist groups and activities; terrorism


Anonymous. "Asahara Ordered Attack," <u>Japan Times Weekly</u> <u>International Edition</u>, 36, No. 39, September 30-October 6, 1996, 1, 6.

At the September 19, 1996, trial hearing of cult leader Shoko Asahara, a former Aum Shinrikyo doctor took the witness stand and testified that he released nerve gas on a Tokyo subway train because he understood the order had been given by the guru. Ikuo Hayashi, a former heart surgeon and chief doctor at the cult's clinic, became the first top Aum leader to testify in the trial of Asahara at the Tokyo District Court. Asahara, whose real name is Chizuo Matsumoto, has been indicted in connection with 17 criminal cases, including the March 1995 nerve gas attack on the Tokyo subway system that left 11 people dead and 3,796 injured. Hayashi has been indicted on six cases, including his involvement in the subway attack. He has pleaded guilty to all the charges against him.

Keyword(s): terrorist cults; terrorist groups and activities; CBRNC; chemical terrorism; chemical attacks; chemical weapons of mass destruction


Anonymous. "Cultist Says He Complied with Gas Attack Out of Fear," <u>Japan Times Weekly International Edition</u>, 38, No. 8, February 23-March 1, 1998, 4.

A senior Aum Shinrikyo figure testified that he did not want to carry out the 1995 sarin gas attack on the Tokyo subway system but was unable to challenge the order for fear of retaliation from the cult.

Keyword(s): CBRNC; chemical weapons of mass destruction; terrorist cults; antiterrorism; combating terrorism; chemical attacks


Anonymous. "Cultists Refuse to Testify against Asahara in Trial," <u>Japan Times Weekly International Edition</u>, 38, No. 43, October 26-November 1, 1998, 4.

Two Aum Shinrikyo figures accused of being involved in the 1994 Matsumoto sarin gas attack took the witness stand for prosecutors at the trial of Aum founder Shoko Asahara on October 15, 1998, but both refused to testify. Tomomitsu Niimi, a key cult figure, said he cannot testify because he refused comment on the case in his own trial. Former Aum chemist Seiichi Endo said he needs to discuss the case further with his lawyers before testifying.

Keyword(s): terrorist cults; CBRNC; chemical attacks; antiterrorism; combating terrorism; chemical weapons of mass destruction

Anonymous. "Hayashi Admits Guilt in Subway Gas Attack," Japan Times Weekly International Edition, 37, No. 27, July 7-13, 1997, 4.

Yasuo Hayashi, a former Aum Shinrikyo fugitive, admitted in court on June 26, 1997, that he released nerve gas in a Tokyo subway car in March 1995. He stated that he could not refuse orders he believed were issued by cult founder Shoko Asahara. A key figure in Aum's science team, Hayashi said he became involved in the crimes at the direction of other Aum senior members, but it was his understanding that the orders came from Asahara.

Keyword(s): terrorism; terrorist cults; CBRNC; chemical weapons of mass destruction; chemical terrorism

Anonymous. "Two Aum Fugitives Arrested," Japan Times Weekly International Edition, 36, No. 47, November 25-December 1, 1996, 1,6.

On November 14, 1996, two Aum Shinrikyo fugitives were arrested in Tokorozawa, Saitama Prefecture, on suspicion of murder and attempted murder. Chief Cabinet Secretary Seiroku Kajiyama announced the arrest of Zenji Yagisawa and Koichi Kitamura at a news conference. Police were planning to question the two about their suspected contacts with five cultists still on a nationwide wanted list, including Yasuo Hayashi, whose alleged role in the March 1995 shooting of National Police Agency chief Takaji Kunimatsu recently came to light. Investigators suspect the five may be hiding in the Tokyo area. Yagisawa turned himself in at a police station in Tokorozawa and was arrested for his alleged role in a foiled cyanide gas attack at Shinjuku Station in May 1995. His statement led to the arrest of Kitamura near a Tokorozawa apartment that the two were renting under false names.

Keyword(s): terrorist cults; terrorist groups and activities; CBRNC; chemical attacks; antiterrorism; combating terrorism; chemical weapons of mass destruction

Hani, Yoko, and Tomoko Otake. "The Trials of Shoko Asahara," Japan Times Weekly International Edition, 38, No. 50, December 14-20, 1998, 7.

Thirty-one months and 99 hearings after Aum Shinrikyo founder Shoko Asahara's trial started, nobody is sure how long it will take before a ruling is made on any of the 17 criminal charges for which he stands accused.

Keyword(s): CBRNC; chemical weapons of mass destruction; terrorist cults; antiterrorism; combating terrorism; terrorism

Howard, Roger. "Entertaining Osama: Testing the Limits of Taliban Hospitality," Jane's Intelligence

Review, [London], 10, No. 11, November 1998, 14-16.

The article asserts that Osama bin Laden is not free to undertake terrorist retaliations against the United States and its "agents" because to do so would cost him the support and sympathy of his Taliban hosts in Afghanistan. The article discusses Bin Laden's relationship with the Taliban regime. It concludes that Bin Laden will not initiate any terrorist reprisal but instead will allow the detailed planning and execution of any terrorist actions to originate elsewhere.

Keyword(s): terrorism; terrorist groups and activities; antiterrorism; combating terrorism; counterterrorism

Israeli, Raphael. "Islamikaze and Their Significance," Terrorism and Political Violence [London], 9, No. 4, Winter 1997, 159-65.

The article analyzes the training, psychology, and philosophical background of Islamic suicide bombers. It attempts to draw conclusions about how and why they commit acts of mass murder.

Keyword(s): terrorist groups and activities; ta; antiterrorism

Mahmood, Cynthia Keppley. Fighting for Faith and Nation: Dialogues with Sikh Militants. Philadelphia: University of Pennsylvania Press, 1997. [Call Number: DS485.P88M25 1997]

The book provides an anthropological study of the origins and structure of Sikh religious militancy. Extensive interviews with expatriate Khalistani militants show the mind set and motivations of the movement. The book also portrays the political system against which the Sikh militants have been struggling since India's independence.

Keyword(s): terrorist groups and activities; terrorist cults

Metraux, Daniel A. "Aum Sweet Home: The Appeal of Aum Shinrikyo to Japan's Restless and Depressed Youth," American Asian Review, 15, Fall 1997, 191-210.

This article examines the history, theology, and membership of the Aum Shinrikyo terrorist cult. It also discusses its founder and leader, Asahara Shoko.

Keyword(s): terrorist cults; terrorism; CBRNC; biological weapons of mass destruction; biological terrorism; chemical terrorism; terrorist groups and activities; chemical weapons of mass destruction

Miller, Judith. "Some in Japan Fear Authors of Subway Attack Are Regaining Ground," New York Times, October 11, 1998, 12.

This in-depth feature on the Aum Shinrikyo terrorist cult in Japan reports that the sect is regrouping, recruiting new members at home and abroad, and raising vast sums of money, partly as a result of Japan's unwillingness to ban it. The group now has about 5,000 members in Japan as well as Ukraine, Belarus, and Kazakhstan. It maintains encrypted Web sites and continues to recruit young scientists, engineers, and other well-educated people.

Keyword(s): terrorist cults; cyberterrorism; CBRNC; terrorist groups and activities

Mutsuko, Murakami. ""The Cult That Won't Die"," Asiaweek, [Hong Kong], 24, no. 50, December 18, 1998, 46-52. [Call Number: DS1.A715]

This article briefly recounts the history of the Aum Shinrikyo cult in Japan in the context of the court proceedings against its guru-leader, Asahara Shokou.

Keyword(s): chemical attacks; terrorist cults

Mylvaganam, Senthil Kumar. "The LTTE: A Regional Problem or a Global Threat?," Crime and Justice International, 14, March 1998, 11-12.

The article discusses the drugs-for-arms trade and other illegal practices of the Liberation of Tamil Tigers (LTTE), a terrorist organization with a Marxist orientation operating in the northern region of Sri Lanka.

Keyword(s): terrorism; terrorist groups and activities; combating terrorism; counterterrorism

Omprakash, S., ed. Terrorism in India. New Delhi: Ess Ess Publications, 1997. [Call Number: HV6433.I4T473 1997]

This volume is the outcome of a symposium on community psychology in present-day Indian society. Nineteen scholars discuss the psychological aspects of terrorism in India, including several who concentrate on Kashmiri and Punjabi terrorism. [lb]

Keyword(s): combating terrorism; counterterrorism; terrorist groups and activities

Otake, Tomoko, and Yoko Hani. "The State vs. Aum," Japan Times Weekly International Edition, 37, No. 6, February 10-16, 1997, 5.

The Japanese Public Security Commission's decision on January 31, 1997, not to invoke the Antisubversive Activities Law against Aum Shinrikyo reflects tremendous changes that the cult has gone through in the past few years, including the arrests of its key figures and fugitives, and its declaration of bankruptcy.

Keyword(s): terrorist cults; terrorist groups and activities; combating terrorism; antiterrorism

Yan, Xuetong. "Terrorism Remains a Significant Threat to Mankind," China Daily, [Beijing], 18, No. 5351, September 23, 1998, 4.

Rather than a recent phenomenon, terrorism has existed for thousands of years. However, some scholars believe that it is the most significant threat to humankind in the post-Cold War era. Explosions by remote-controlled bombs are the main method used by terrorists. The technology of remote-control bombing is becoming easier to access for terrorists. Such explosions make it possible for terrorists to escape. The author, a research fellow with the China Institute of Contemporary International Relations, believes that with more international entities regarding terrorism as an immoral activity there will be little room for terrorists to act.

Keyword(s): technology; terrorism (general); radio frequency weapons; antiterrorism; combating terrorism

Zurer, Pamela. "Japanese Cult Used VX to Slay Member," Chemical and Engineering News, 76, No. 35, August 31, 1998, 7.

The Aum Shinrikyo sect murdered one of its own members with the deadly nerve agent VX, according to a Japanese forensic toxicologist. The article provides the chemical composition of the VX agent found in the Japanese murder victim. Two cult members sprinkled the nerve agent on the victim's neck in a street in Osaka in 1994, and the victim died 10 days later.

Keyword(s): technology; CBRNC; chemical weapons of mass destruction; chemical terrorism; chemical, biological, nuclear agents; terrorist cults; chemical attacks

## Europe

Anonymous. "'Intelligent' EDS Passes FAA Muster," Airports International, 31, No. 4, May 1998, 30.

The article notes the Federal Aviation Administration's approval of the CTX 5500 explosives detection system, made by InVision Technologies, which provides continuous monitoring of baggage as it passes through a terminal. The new concept of dynamic screening also is adaptable to different threat levels and airport conditions and offers improved computer hardware and software. Anticipated applications at various airports and in various countries are noted.

Keyword(s): technology; antiterrorism; inspection of aircraft carry-on luggage; inspection of overseas containers

Anonymous. "EuropScan Prepares for Smart X-ray Demonstrations," Airports International, June 1995, 19.

The article announces a testing phase of the French EuropScan "smart" automatic explosive x-ray detection system at Charles de Gaulle Airport in Paris. The history of the system's development is given briefly, with some information on the technical advantages and likely deployment of the "smart" systems around the world. Also discussed is the competition among German and French companies for the market in security detection devices for such places as airports.

Keyword(s): technology; antiterrorism; inspection of carry-on luggage; inspection of aircraft cargo containers

Anonymous. "Safety and Security: EG&G Astrophysics," Airports International, 30, No. 7, September 1997, 55-56.

The article notes the use by Manchester Airport (England) of Z-Scan 7 as a step toward achieving 100 percent hold baggage screening. The processing specifications of the systems are given. The article also lists several new pieces of screening technology, including the TSS 2000, which provides the highest level of comprehensive hold baggage screening available at the time of writing.

Keyword(s): technology; antiterrorism; inspection of aircraft cargo containers; inspection of carry-on luggage

Anonymous. "UK Debut for Advanced Security System," Airports International, May 1996, 17-18.

The article describes the development and testing of a new airport security system that combines x-ray and quadruple resonance technology. The system was developed by combining instruments from EG&G Astrophysics and the Quantum Magnetics companies. Also provided is some information on test results and prospective applications of the new equipment.

Keyword(s): technology; inspection of aircraft cargo containers; inspection of aircraft carry-on luggage


Anonymous. "Can of Worms," Crossborder Monitor, 6, No. 48, December 2, 1998, 4.

The arrest in Italy of suspected terrorist Abdullah Ocalan, leader of the Kurdistan Workers' Party, is making waves in Turkey, Europe, and farther afield. Turkey wants to send him back for trial, but Ocalan is seeking political asylum. Italy has freed him pending consideration of a German arrest warrant.

Keyword(s): terrorism; antiterrorism; combating terrorism


Arkin, William M. "No Points Safe," Bulletin of the Atomic Scientists, 54, No. 1, January/February 1998, 73.

The writer discusses the claim in One Point Safe, by Andrew and Leslie Cockburn, that, on January 4, 1977, terrorists mounted a midnight raid against a U.S. nuclear stockpile in Germany. The writer, who was a U.S. Army intelligence analyst serving in West Berlin at the time, asserts that, although a Baader-Meinhof spin-off organization called the Revolutionary Cells planted a bomb on an unmanned fuel storage tank at the Giessen Army Depot, there was no attack on the exclusion area where nuclear weapons were stored. He also maintains that there is no evidence the group knew or cared about nuclear weapons.

Keyword(s): CBRNC; terrorist groups and activities; nuclear weapons of mass destruction


Baldwin, Frank. "Screening Partnership," Airports International, January-February 1996, 13-14.

The article describes the genesis and principles of Britain's policy of 100 percent inspection of all baggage passing through its airports, no matter what its destination or origin. An especially big issue, the attitudes and fears of the airlines toward security procedures, is described in detail, as is the solution to the issue of system cost, as they relate to the attainment of 100 percent hold baggage screening (HBS).

Keyword(s): technology; antiterrorism; inspection of aircraft cargo containers; inspection of carry-on luggage


Barrett, Neil. Digital Crime: Policing the Cybernation. London: Kogan Page, 1997.

The book examines the range of crimes being committed as a result of the technology boom, and ways in which the police and the courts are responding in Britain. It covers gathering and presenting digital information as evidence for prosecution, cyberterrorism and cyberwar, and Internet problems. The growth of encryption and the increase in available processing power has made it difficult to crack the messages of on-line criminals, while simultaneously opening up possibilities for intercepting and hijacking legitimate messages for the purposes of blackmail. The trans-jurisdictional nature of the Internet impedes effective responses by national authorities.

Keyword(s): technology; cyberterrorism; information warfare; combating terrorism; antiterrorism; cyberwar


Bodansky, Yossef. "Italy Becomes Iran's New Base for Terrorist Operations," Defense and Foreign Affairs Strategic Policy, 26, No. 4/5, April 1998, 5-9.

The writer discusses how Iranian Islamists have established an effective terrorist infrastructure in the Balkans region. A forward operations center in Milan, Italy, is preparing to export terror into Western Europe, and this clandestine web has already attempted the assassination of Pope John Paul II.

Keyword(s): terrorism; terrorist groups and activities; combating terrorism; counterterrorism; antiterrorism


Bolle, Pierre-Henri, Andre Sibille, Bernhard Restel, et alia. "La police en interfaces: Colloque universitaire de l'Institut Suisse de Police," Revue Internationale de Criminologie et de Police Technique, [Geneva], 50, No. 2, 1997 [in French], 133-206.

This publication contains the proceedings of two colloquia held in 1996 in honor of the 50th anniversary of the Swiss Police Institute. The second colloquium, on "Europe Horizon 2000: New Threats, New Terrorism," includes the following papers: the theme topic, by Marie-Elisabeth Cartier and Xavier Raufer; mafia-type organizations, by Feliciano Marruzzor; terrorism and narcotrafficking by the Labor Party of Kurdistan, by Francois Haut; money and terrorism, by Rene Wack; the judicial response, by Francois Falletti; and a conclusion, by Jacques Fourvel.

Keyword(s): antiterrorism; combating terrorism; terrorism


Chalk, Peter. West European Terrorism and Counter-Terrorism: The Evolving Dynamic. New York: St. Martin's Press, 1996. [Call Number: HV6433.E85C43 1996]

The chapter provides historical background on terrorist activities in Western Europe prior to the 1990s, then describes new and ongoing trends in several problem areas: Northern Ireland, right-wing extremism in the U.S., militant Islamic fundamentalism, and new separatist groups. Contributing factors such as arms proliferation in Europe and the relaxation of national borders in the European Union also are discussed.

Keyword(s): terrorism; terrorist groups and activities


Dartnell, Michael. "Alias 'GBGPGS': Action Directe Internationale's Transition from Revolutionary Terrorism to Euro-Terrorism," Terrorism and Political Violence, [London], 9, No. 4, Winter 1997, 33-57.

This article discusses terrorism as a ritual act or series of acts expressing a message. The case of the Groupe-Bakounine-Gdansk-Paris-Guatemala-Salvador (GBGPGS) illustrates how complex such messages are by referring them to their French and global contexts. The group's violent struggle against political rules has a "sacrificial" dimension and was justified as a response to "crisis." Through attempting to reinterpret French extreme-left traditions, the GBGPGS campaign foreshadowed Euro-terrorism. The most salient evidence of this shift was the group's concentration on economic globalization and the weakening of traditional state and great-power structures.

Keyword(s): terrorism; terrorist groups and activities; counterterrorism; combating terrorism

Dyson, Ben. "A Question of Capacity," ReActions, [London], 18, No. 11, November 1998, 46-48.

Pool Re, Britain's government-backed terrorism reinsurance operation, has been accused of being inflexible, expensive, and hidebound, yet it survives. Pool Re will not change its policy of covering a company's entire list of premises instead of individual premises because to do so would, it maintains, destroy the existing system. Its members offer terrorism cover at a price specified by Pool Re. Individual rates would mean individual companies setting the price. But Pool Re's rivals believe that its services are still relevant.

Keyword(s): terrorism; antiterrorism; combating terrorism

Goddard, Sarah. "U.K.'s Pool Re to Slash Rates," Business Insurance, [London], 32, No. 43, October 26, 1998, 65, 69.

In 1998 Pool Reinsurance Company, Ltd., the government-backed reinsurer of Britain's mainland terrorism risks, announced that it was considering reviewing premium rates in the wake of the historic Stormont Agreement signed in Northern Ireland on April 10. The agreement potentially ends a conflict that has spilled onto the British mainland for decades. In the absence of terrorism claims over the previous two years, the reinsurer already had discounted premiums by 20 percent for properties in cities and 40 percent for properties elsewhere from the beginning of 1998. Economic Secretary to the Treasury Patricia Hewitt has announced that 1999 premiums will be discounted by 85 percent on average, reflecting the recent lack of losses.

Keyword(s): antiterrorism; combating terrorism; terrorism

Hodges, Kim. "A Dog for All Reasons," Airports International, 30, No. 8, October 1997, 14-16.

The article outlines the present use of dogs for explosives detection in Europe's larger airports such as Heathrow and Frankfurt. The advantages and techniques of sniffer dogs are discussed, with information on the training and application of dogs at specific airports. The article also evaluates the future role of dogs in view of more sophisticated concealment methods, with mention of a new biosensory "artificial nose" planned by Bofors of Sweden, but the conclusion is that dogs provide a uniquely flexible and sensitive approach to the problem.

Keyword(s): technology; explosives detection; inspection of carry-on luggage; inspection of aircraft passengers

Holland, Jack, and Susan Phoenix. Phoenix: Policing the Shadows: The Secret War against Terrorism in Northern Ireland. London: Hodder, 1996.

This book examines undercover operations conducted by the police and British armed and security forces and intelligence services against the Irish Republican Army (IRA), and secret negotiations that led to the IRA cease-fire. The book is based on the life of Royal Ulster Constabulary (RUC) Detective Superintendent Ian Phoenix. Also examined are counterterrorism operations by Britain's Special Air Service (SAS), the struggle between the Northern Ireland Special Branch and MI5 for control of top secret information channels, and other topics.

Keyword(s): counterterrorism; combating terrorism; terrorism

Kemp, Damian. "UK Bio-Agent Detector System Is Delivered," Jane's Defence Weekly, 31, No. 2, January 13, 1999, 17.

Britain's Ministry of Defence has accepted the vehicle-mounted Prototype Biological Detection System (PBDS), which builds on the technology of a basic Biological Detection System (BDS). British forces used the BDS during the 1990-91 Gulf War. The PBDS provides a deployable detection capability to provide field commanders with information to institute protective and medical countermeasures. The PBDS will provide the basis for a more advanced Integrated Biological Detection System (IBDS).

Keyword(s): biological agent detection; technology; combating terrorism; antiterrorism

Kielman, Maria. "Terrorism Coverage Expands in Academia," Business Insurance, [London], 32, No. 40, October 5, 1998, 57-58.

British academic institutions are obtaining more terrorism coverage at less cost through a unique mutual insurance facility. UM Association (Terrorism) Ltd. (UMALT) was established in 1993 to provide British academic institutions with an alternative to the British government's terrorism insurance program.

Keyword(s): antiterrorism; combating terrorism; terrorism

Lorenzini, Sara. "La Convenzione di Ginevra per l'Istituzione di una Corte Penale Internazionale sul Terrorismo: Un document da tornare a leggere," Il Politico, [Rome], 62, January-March 1997, 115-29.

The article discusses reasons why Italy decided not to accede to the Geneva Convention for the establishment of an international criminal court to try persons accused of acts of terrorism, opened for signing at the League of Nations on November 16, 1937. The article includes the text of the Convention, which was not signed and ratified by enough countries to permit its entry into force.

Keyword(s): antiterrorism; combating terrorism; terrorism

Machlis, Sharon. "E-Mail Bombings Shut Down Site," Computerworld, 31, No. 30, July 28, 1997, 6.

The Institute for Global Communications (IGC) in July 1997 was hit with hundreds of electronic-mail bombs and other denial-of-service attacks because it hosted a site that promoted Basque independence. The Web attack likely came from Spaniards upset that the Web site had information about Euskadi Ta Askatasuma (ETA), a Basque separatist group that has carried out a campaign of assassination and bombings for many years. The IGC received many legitimate complaints about the Basque site, but also faced organized, malicious attacks designed not to communicate with anyone, but simply to make its computers unusable. The vigilante attack on IGC may actually be a bigger problem than censorship by governments, because Internet service providers (ISPs) have no recourse against a vigilante attack.

Keyword(s): cyberterrorism; information warfare; combating terrorism; antiterrorism; terrorist groups and activities; terrorism


Merkl, Peter H.. "Radical Right Parties in Europe and Anti-Foreign Violence: A Comparative Essay," Terrorism and Political Violence [London], 7, No. 1, Spring 1995, 96-118.

The article analyzes violence committed against perceived foreigners in European countries, including the historical background of such activity. It places such activity in the context of more organized terrorist groups, identifying its sociological and fundamentally non-political basis. The relationship between individual acts and a community's general hostility toward outsiders also is examined.

Keyword(s): terrorist groups and activities; terrorism (general)


Paris, Henri. "La menace terroriste et insurrectionnelle," Defense Nationale, [Paris], 54, April 1998, 45-56.

This article examines terrorist threats to internal security in France, as well as social unrest and violence in general. It discusses the situation in big cities and among certain segments of the population, including inhabitants of high-rise neighborhoods and the unemployed, the failure of educational and military organizations in their role to help assimilation of disadvantaged groups, and terrorist influences from foreign sources.

Keyword(s): terrorism; antiterrorism; combating terrorism


Pluchinsky, Dennis A. "Terrorism in the Former Soviet Union: A Primer, A Puzzle, A Prognosis," Studies in Conflict and Terrorism, [London], 21, No. 2, April-June 1998, 119-47.

This article examines political terrorist activity in the 15 newly independent states of the former Soviet Union and the problems that security and terrorism analysts will encounter when assessing this activity. It introduces the reader to a form of terrorism known as "blood-feud terrorism." The geographic focus of the article is the southern Russian republics of Dagestan, Chechnya, Ingushetia, and North Ossetia; the regions of Abkhazia and Marneuli in Georgia; Azerbaijan; and Tajikistan. Collectively, these areas have the potential of replacing the Middle East as the primary generator of international crises and international terrorism. The article includes seven maps and a chronology of selected political terrorist incidents in the former Soviet Union, 1995-97.

Keyword(s): terrorism; terrorist groups and activities

Politi, Alessandro. "European Security: The New Transnational Risks," West European Union Institute for Security Studies, Chaillot papers, No. 29, 1997, entire issue.

The paper discusses the contemporary status of international terrorism in Europe and changes brought by the establishment of the European Union and consequent changes in transnational monitoring. Also discussed is the current debate over international authority and effective antiterrorist organization in this light, including the possible use of multinational military organizations.

Keyword(s): terrorist groups and activities; future trends; antiterrorism

Preston, Richard. "The Bioweaponeers," New Yorker, 74, No. 3, March 9, 1998, 52-65.

In the last few years, Russian scientists have invented the world's deadliest plagues, including the Alibekov anthrax developed by the former first deputy chief of research and production for the Soviet biological-weapons program, Ken Alibek (formerly Kanatjan Alibekov). Alibek and Bill Patrick, the oldest United Nations weapons inspector in Iraq, discuss the power of anthrax and the possibility of bioterrorism.

Keyword(s): technology; CBRNC; chemical weapons of mass destruction; chemical terrorism; biological terrorism; biological weapons of mass destruction

Shaw, Douglas, and William Alberque. "Cooperative Efforts to Prevent the Terrorist Acquisition of Nuclear Materials from Russia, the New Independent States, and the Baltics," Low Intensity Conflict and Law Enforcement, [London], 6, No. 2, Autumn 1997, 169-78.

The possibility that terrorists could acquire and use a nuclear weapon is increasingly hard to exclude in the post-Cold War world, in the assessment of the authors. The dissolution of the Soviet Union has created new challenges for protecting nuclear material. The article discusses cooperative efforts in this regard being undertaken between the United States, on the one hand, and Russia, the newly independent states, and the Baltic states, on the other. The authors, who are employees of the Department of Energy, believe that their department's cooperative program has demonstrated concrete results in the level of trust and close cooperation that it has been able to develop with the scientists of the cooperating countries.

Keyword(s): CBRNC; nuclear terrorism; biological weapons of mass destruction; biological terrorism; chemical terrorism; combating terrorism; counterterrorism; chemical weapons of mass destruction

Silke, Andrew. "In Defense of the Realm: Financing Loyalist Terrorism in Northern Ireland--Part One:

15

Extortion and Blackmail," <u>Studies in Conflict and Terrorism</u>, 21, No. 5, September-October 1998, 331-61.

The revival of loyalist terrorism has been one of the most important developments in Northern Ireland in the 1990s. This article examines the recent fund-raising activities of the two main loyalist paramilitary groups, the Ulster Defence Association (UDA) and the Ulster Volunteer Force (UVF). The article focuses particularly on the financial importance of extortion and blackmail to the groups in the 1990s. It also explores how the loyalist paramilitaries have responded, as organizations, to the constant need for funds. This need has continued unabated since both groups implemented cease-fires in 1994. The article concludes that because of internal arrangements, the loyalist groups are consistently risking the spread of corruption among their most senior members.

Keyword(s): terrorism; terrorist groups and activities

Venter, Al J. "Sverdlovsk Outbreak: A Portent of Disaster," <u>Jane's Intelligence Review</u>, [London], 10, No. 5, May 1998, 36-41.

Since several terrorist groups, including Japan's Aum Shinrikyo cult, have experimented with anthrax, some authorities now maintain that the prospect of an anthrax attack is more a question of when, rather than if. Tests have shown that the number of people subjected to weaponized, aerosol-disseminated anthrax spores could be reckoned in terms of hundreds of thousands. The article examines the anthrax outbreak in Sverdlovsk in 1979. It also discusses the potential use of anthrax as a terrorist and biological warfare weapon.

Keyword(s): biological terrorism; CBRNC; biological weapons of mass destruction; weapons of mass destruction in urban areas; biological agent detection

Vorobiev, Alexander. "Countering Chemical/Biological Terrorism in the Former Soviet Union: The Need for Cooperative Efforts," <u>Politics and the Life Sciences</u>, [London], 15, September 1996, 233-5.

This article is a commentary on Jonathan B. Tucker's "Chemical/Biological Terrorism: Coping with a New Threat" (see Tucker, Jonathan B.). To a certain extent, Tucker's article refers to the existing situation in the former Soviet Union, but Alexander Vorobiev contributes some additional thoughts on that matter as well as on potential international cooperative efforts. He describes the legislative base that was established in Russia to deny possible access by terrorist states and terrorist groups to CBRNC, dual-use technologies, and materials.

Keyword(s): CBRNC; chemical weapons of mass destruction; biological weapons of mass destruction; chemical terrorism; biological terrorism; counterterrorism; combating terrorism

Weinberg, Leonard. "Italian Neo-Fascist Terrorism: A Comparative Perspective," <u>Terrorism and Political Violence [London]</u>, 7, No. 1, Spring 1995, 221-38.

The article analyzes the methodology and goals of postwar Italian terrorism in the context of other European groups and movements. The analysis compares targets, methodology, political rationales, and goals, identifying significant, long-term differences between the Italian groups and others in Europe.

Keyword(s): terrorist groups and activities; terrorism (general)

## International

Adams, James. <u>The Next World War: Computers Are the Weapons and</u> the Front Line Is Everywhere. New York: Simon and Schuster, 1998. [Call Number: U163 .A33 1998]

The author, who is a veteran defense journalist and chief executive officer of United Press International (UPI), examines war in the information age. Drawing on the voluminous periodical literature, he discusses the threat posed by cyberterrorists. This new breed of terrorists can, at least in theory, paralyze financial systems and cause horrible industrial accidents with a few keystrokes. The author also meditates on the effects of instantaneous worldwide news and provides examples of technologically sophisticated fiction. He concludes that "America today looks uncomfortably like Goliath, arrogant in its power, armed to the teeth, ignorant of its weakness."

Keyword(s): cyberterrorism; antiterrorism; counterterrorism; technology; information warfare; combating terrorism

Alexander, Lexi. <u>Decontaminating Civilian Facilities: Biological Agents and Toxins</u>. Institute for Defense Analysis, 1998.

This report reviews current (1997-98) processes and procedures for decontaminating the interior of a public building or transportation system following a terrorist release of a biological agent and/or a toxin within. Attempting to provide a template for handling such a disaster, Alexander outlines how such an event should be handled--from technical issues to agency responsibilities.

Keyword(s): antiterrorism; combating terrorism; CBRNC; biological weapons of mass destruction; biological decontamination; chemical/biological decontamination; biological terrorism

Allison, Graham T., Owen R. Cote, Jr., Richard A. Falkenrath, and Steven E. Miller. <u>Avoiding Nuclear Anarchy: Containing the Threat of Loose Russian Nuclear Weapons and Fissile Material</u>. Cambridge, Massachusetts and London: MIT Press, 1996. [Call Number: HV6431.A96 1996]

The book addresses the problem of controlling the nuclear weapons remaining in post-Soviet Russia under questionable security conditions of what the authors call an ongoing revolution in that country. The book describes the threat of nuclear terrorist attack in the U.S. that is increased under these conditions and it offers possible policy solutions to the problem.

Keyword(s): nuclear terrorism; future trends; antiterrorism

American Banker. "Cyber Terrorism," <u>American Banker Future Banking Supplement</u>, 1, No. 6, September 1997, 43-45.

According to The Times of London, several London financial institutions had paid as much as 400 million pounds in 1996 to fend off extortionists using software programs causing systematic errors. There are no laws for banks coming under cyberattack, for there are no national boundaries. According to a table on the results of a survey on computer crime and security, the number of reported computer-related incidents were 2,573 in 1996 versus 2,412 in 1995 and 2,341 in 1994. A 1997 study by San Francisco's Computer Security Institute said that the 249 respondents reported losses of $100,119,555. Of that, $65,623,700 was for system penetration, sabotage, virus attacks, fraud, and theft of proprietary information.

Keyword(s): technology; cyberterrorism

Anderson, Sean K. "Warnings Versus Alarms: Terrorist Threat Analysis Applied to the Iranian State-Run Media," Studies in Conflict and Terrorism, [London], 21, No. 3, July 1998, 277-305.

Keyword(s): State-sponsored terrorism is a form of coercion, backed up by the threat and use of violence, to achieve political ends. These terrorist tactics also involve signaling of intentions and responses between the terrorist sponsor and those whom it targets.

Anonymous. "Heimann Close to Placing Smart System," Airports International, July-August 1995, 20.

The article describes the role of the German Heimann Systems company in "smart" explosives detection to accommodate the commercial airports' need for 100 percent x-ray screening of baggage. The international sales activities of Heimann in airport security devices are described, including its exclusive agreement to supply detection systems to all of Germany's airports and to provide operator training in some cases.

Keyword(s): antiterrorism; inspection of aircraft cargo containers; inspection of carry-on luggage

Anonymous. "InVision Broadens Horizons," Airports International, 30, No. 4, May 1997, 12.

The article reports the purchase by the Kuala Lumpur International Airport of six CTX 5000 explosives detection system units, as well as applications in Chicago and New York and several European and Asian locations. Specific configurations in Chicago and New York are provided.

Keyword(s): Explosives detection; inspection of aircraft cargo containers; inspection of carry-on luggage

Anonymous. "Demand for Detection Devices Skyrockets," Canadian Electronics, 13, No. 4, June 1998, 8.

Because of the heightened awareness of chemical and biological weapons, worldwide spending on chemical-biological (CB) defense equipment continues to rise. The world demand for chemical warfare agent detectors is estimated to grow an average of 12 percent through the forecast period 1998-2005, comprising the majority of the overall market in CB warfare agent detection.

Keyword(s): antiterrorism; combating terrorism; CBRNC; chemical weapons of mass destruction; technology; biological agent detection; biological weapons of mass destruction

Anonymous. "Anthrax to Zyklon-B: A Deadly Alphabet," Drug Topics, 142, No. 6, March 16, 1998, 46.

Anthrax has been the most notorious biological agent in the news in 1998. However, it is just one of many potential weapons of the biochemical terrorist. Others include bubonic plague, ricin, sarin, vesicants, and Zyklon-B.

Keyword(s): CBRNC; chemical weapons of mass destruction; antiterrorism; biological agent detection; combating terrorism; biological weapons of mass destruction

Anonymous. "Terrorism: Computer Flaw Threatens Airport Security," Facts on File World News Digest, October 16, 1998, 1-2.

A California-based computer consultant found a major flaw in a computerized security system used in some U.S. and British airports, according to a story in the New York Times datelined February 7, 1998. The glitch would allow terrorists to penetrate security in airports. The system, made by Receptors Inc. in Torrance, California, used electronic badges to limit access to secured areas in airports and other institutions. The consulting firm, MSB Associates, determined that the system could be manipulated by an intruder via telephone lines or a computer network. By dialing into the system's central computer, a person could create unauthorized badges and erase evidence of their use. The same technique could be used to unlock doors to secured areas.

Keyword(s): technology; cyberterrorism; document analysis; antiterrorism; combating terrorism; recognition of personnel

Anonymous. "Keeping Terrorists at Bay," Futurist, 32, No. 9, December 1998, 15.
The number of terrorist incidents in the world increased more than 300 percent in the last three decades, according to Peace Watch magazine, and it is getting worse. The best solution is to deny terrorists the expertise that they need. A current U.S. government program finds alternative employment for scientists from the former Soviet Union, preventing experts who understand nuclear, chemical, and biological weapons from selling their skills to extremist groups.

Keyword(s): future trends; terrorism; antiterrorism; combating terrorism; CBRNC

Anonymous. "HHS Awards $9.2 Million for Medical Strike Teams," Healthcare Financial Management, 51, No. 11, November 1997, 21-22.

The Department of Health and Human Services (HHS) is awarding $9.2 million in contracts to 25 cities for development of specialized strike teams to provide medical care in the event of nuclear, chemical, or biological terrorism. The teams, known as Metropolitan Medical Strike Teams, are designed to provide initial on-site response and safe patient transportation to hospital emergency departments in the event of a terrorist attack.

Keyword(s): first responders; combating terrorism; CBRNC; chemical weapons of mass destruction; biological weapons of mass destruction; nuclear terrorism; chemical terrorism; biological terrorism; antiterrorism

Anonymous. "Real Threat of Bioterrorism Discussed in Atlanta," Lancet, 351, No. 9106, March 21, 1998, 887.

More and more nations are experimenting with biological weapons. The threat of bioterrorism was discussed at the International Conference on Emerging Infectious Diseases in Atlanta, Georgia.

Keyword(s): future trends; CBRNC; biological weapons of mass destruction; biological terrorism

Anonymous. "Bioterrorism Special Report: Firm but Fair," New Scientist, [London], 157, February 28, 1998, 4-6.

The article discusses the importance of the March 1998 meeting of the Biological and Toxin Weapons Convention (BTWC), noting that the world still has no means of checking on whether countries are keeping their BTWC promises. The example of Iraq has shown how even a relatively undeveloped country can produce an impressive biological arsenal in secret. The article editorializes that the United States, which rejects random inspections, should let the inspectors in, despite the concerns of the biotechnology firms. It also emphasizes the need for stricter controls on trade in potentially dangerous biological organisms.

Keyword(s): CBRNC; biological weapons of mass destruction; antiterrorism; combating terrorism; biological terrorism

Anonymous. "Coping with Terrorism," Peace Watch, 4, No. 6, October 1998, 1-3.

The article summarizes a panel discussion of a paper, "Counterterrorism Strategy: Lessons after Nairobi, Dar es-Salaam, and Omagh," given by Ehud Sprinzak at a U.S. Institute of Peace current issues briefing on August 26, 1998. The event was moderated by Robert Oakley of the National Defense University. The panel addressed the question: Should a state respond to terrorist attacks with force or seek to address root causes through political dialogue? According to panelist Paul Arthur, a security response often galvanizes terrorist movements or drives sympathetic elements of a society to support it. Sprinzak noted that terrorism is a form of psychological warfare.

Keyword(s): combating terrorism; counterterrorism; antiterrorism

Anonymous. "The New Terrorists," Peace Watch, 4, No. 4, June 1998, 6-7.

Terrorist incidents have increased internationally more than 300 percent in the past three decades, escalating from 8,114 incidents in the 1970s to more than 27,000 in 1990-96. According to Jessica Stern, a former member of the National Security Council and an expert on nuclear, biological, and chemical weapons, "a small but increasing number of terrorists is interested in using weapons of mass destruction." She adds: "There have been only about 10 cases in which materials seized by law enforcement authorities in an attempted theft or smuggling were weapons-usable nuclear materials."

Keyword(s): terrorism; terrorist groups and activities; nuclear weapons of mass destruction; nuclear terrorism; CBRNC

Anonymous. "The Top Ten," Security Management, 41, No. 4, April 1997, 30.

Terrorist groups vary greatly in size, longevity, and sophistication. No more than ten groups in any single year individually launch more than ten attacks. Most terrorist groups conduct fewer than five attacks in any given year. U.S. statistics show that Islamic radical fundamentalists are not and have not been the most active terrorist groups. The record-holder is a Kurdish-Marxist group called the Kurdistan Workers' Party (PKK). However, the data for 1995 show an increase in radical Islamic groups in the top ten compared with the groups most active from 1991 to 1995. The Islamic radical fundamentalists are clearly the most deadly terrorist groups.

Keyword(s): terrorism (general); antiterrorism; counterterrorism; terrorist groups and activities; combating terrorism

Babievsky, Kirill K.. "Chemical and Biological Terrorism," Low Intensity Conflict and Law Enforcement, [London], 6, No. 2, Autumn 1997, 163-68.

This article provides some brief historical perspective on incidents of chemical/biological (CB) terrorism. It finds that an analysis of 200 incidents of CB terrorism shows seven broad categories of adversaries and their percentage. For example, 20 percent were politically motivated, 9 percent were acting as agents of a sovereign state, and 7 percent were motivated by philosophical or religious considerations. The article also discusses various types of CB terrorism threats and the need to supplement the 1993 Chemical Weapons Convention with improved intelligence collection and monitoring, an expanded civil defense program, and realistic recovery plans.

Keyword(s): CBRNC; biological weapons of mass destruction; chemical weapons of mass destruction; biological terrorism; chemical terrorism; counterterrorism; antiterrorism; combating terrorism

Badey, Thomas J. "Defining International Terrorism: A Pragmatic Approach," Terrorism and Political Violence, [London], 10, No. 1, Spring 1998, 90-107.

Despite a plethora of scholarly work and more than 30 years of intergovernmental discourse, there is still no commonly accepted definition of international terrorism. Existing definitions tend to fall into two broad categories--academic and political. Contemporary academic definitions of international terrorism are designed primarily to fit incidents into various statistical models. Defying common usage, they are often lengthy and over-complicated. Governmental definitions of international terrorism tend to be ambiguous to allow the most politically convenient interpretation of events. This paper examines the ongoing definitional dilemma in the study of international terrorism. Drawing on both sides of the definitional spectrum, it charts a middle course, arguing for a more lucid and functional definition based on primary characteristics that distinguish international terrorism from other types of violence.

Keyword(s): terrorism; antiterrorism; combating terrorism

Bailey, Kathleen C. "Policy Options for Combatting Chemical/Biological Terrorism," Politics and the Life Sciences, [London], 15, September 1996, 185-87.

This article is a commentary on Jonathan B. Tucker's "Chemical/Biological Terrorism: Coping with a New Threat," which appears in this issue (see Tucker, Jonathan B.). The writer argues that although Tucker offers an excellent review of the threat of chemical/biological (C/B) terrorism, his article is somewhat weak on the issue of what measures should be taken in anticipation of and in response to such attacks. Bailey offers a critique of some of Tucker's suggestions, cites a number of the U.S. Government's current efforts to address C/B terrorism, and suggests further options.

Keyword(s): biological terrorism; chemical terrorism; biological weapons of mass destruction; chemical weapons of mass destruction; antiterrorism; combating terrorism

Ballentyne, George. "The Terrorist Use of Weapons of Mass Destruction," Newsbrief, [London], 18:6 (June 1998), 46-48.

The author considers the danger posed to the world by the proliferation of nuclear technology and weapons of mass destruction and asks why they have been employed in so few terrorist incidents during the last 30 years. He notes the difficulties of obtaining and handling such weapons as among the reasons for their lack of use by individual terrorist groups. He argues that leaders or subnational groups within sovereign nation states who possess weapons of mass destruction are most likely to use them in the future, citing Nazi Germany and Iraq during the Iran-Iraq War as examples. The absence of such weapons from national arsenals would be the best way to ensure that they are not used by rogue leaders and groups. lb

Keyword(s): CBRNC; biological weapons of mass destruction; chemical weapons of mass destruction; nuclear terrorism; future trends

Beal, Clifford. "Facing the Invisible Enemy," Jane's Defence Weekly, [London], 30, No. 18, November 1998, 23-26.

The article focuses on the threat of chemical and biological warfare (CBW) agents delivered by ballistic or cruise missiles in a wartime situation and the countermeasures being accelerated by the United States and Britain. The article discusses specific detection systems being developed to counter the threat.

Keyword(s): combating terrorism; counterterrorism; biological terrorism; CBRNC; chemical terrorism;

biological agent detection; chemical weapons of mass destruction; biological weapons of mass destruction

Binder, Patrice. "Biological/Chemical Terrorism: The Threat and Possible Countermeasures," <u>Politics and the Life Sciences</u>, [London], 15, September 1996, 188-9.

This article is a commentary on Jonathan B. Tucker's "Chemical/Biological Terrorism: Coping with a New Threat" (see Tucker, Jonathan B.). The writer argues that Tucker makes a constructive bid to examine the potential threat of chemical and biological terrorism. Binder contends that present-day terrorists can be divided into three groups: individuals or groups with political aims, nihilists, and religious fanatics or sect adherents motivated by very strong ideologies without clear political objectives. He argues that the possibility for biological and chemical terrorism cannot be ignored and that the international community needs to concentrate on fundamentalist religious groups and other sects that could be the most likely users of such weapons. He concludes that domestic management through relevant legislation on the manipulation and circulation of biological produce could be a first step toward deterring and revealing potential users.

Keyword(s): biological terrorism; chemical terrorism; antiterrorism; biological weapons of mass destruction; chemical weapons of mass destruction; antiterrorism; combating terrorism; biological agent detection

Bjorgo, Tore, ed. <u>Terror from the Extreme Right</u>. London: Frank Cass, 1995. [Call Number: HV6432.T44 1995]

The book is a series of essays characterizing various international terrorist groups with right-wing political agendas, their philosophies and patterns of operation. It provides extensive accounts of attacks and documentation of xenophobic and ethocentric justifications by the groups. In describing specific groups, the book also provides typical patterns of behavior for various types of right-wing terrorist organization.

Keyword(s): terrorist groups and activities; terrorism (general)

Blum, William. "Anthrax for Export," <u>The Progressive</u>, 62, No. 4, April 1998, 18-20.

The United States supplied Iraq with much of the raw material for creating a chemical and biological warfare program. U.S. companies sold Iraq more than $1 billion worth of the components needed to build nuclear weapons and diverse types of missiles. When Iraq engaged in chemical and biological warfare in the 1980s, the United States kept supplying it with the materials it needed to build weapons. The article details the biological and chemical materials sold to Iraq by U.S. companies from 1985 through 1989 and lists the specific companies.

Keyword(s): biological terrorism; CBRNC; biological weapons of mass destruction; chemical weapons of mass destruction; nuclear weapons of mass destruction; combating terrorism; antiterrorism; biological weapons of mass destruction

Bowers, Stephen R., and Kimberly R. Keys. "Technology and Terrorism: The New Threat for the Millennium," Conflict Studies, [London], No. 300, May 1998, 1-24.

The article discusses the imminent threats posed by the emergence and active proliferation of computer, biological, and chemical terrorism as a consequence of technological innovations, as well as the security threat posed by nontraditional, namely nonstate and transitional, actors. Related topics examined also include the cyberterrorist potential, biological and chemical weapons and agents, and indications and warning systems.

Keyword(s): CBRNC; biological terrorism; biological weapons of mass destruction; chemical terrorism; chemical weapons of mass destruction; cyberterrorism

Brill, Arthur P., Jr. "Blessed Are the Gatekeepers," Sea Power, 41, No. 11, November 1998, 43-45.

The United States Marine Corps's Marine Security Guards (MSGs) serve as the "front line defense" at U.S. embassies worldwide. MSGs have often been the victims of terrorist attacks, including recent bombings. The topics discussed include armed forces, military personnel, diplomatic and consular services, security, and U.S. international relations.

Keyword(s): antiterrorism; combating terrorism; terrorism; counterterrorism

Builta, Jeffrey A., John Murray, and Richard H. Ward. Extremist Groups: An International Compilation of Terrorist Organizations, Violent Political Groups and Issue-Oriented Militant Movements. Chicago, Illinois: Office of International Criminal Justice, University of Illinois, 1996.

This compendium, based on secondary or open-source materials, lists what is known about goals, areas of operation, structure, funding, types of activities, and significant actions undertaken by groups that espouse violence or display the threat of violence in their pursuit of political goals. Some 250 groups are listed by geographic region.

Keyword(s): terrorism; ad hoc and transient terrorist groups; terrorist groups and activities; terrorist cults

Burck, Gordon M. "New Terrorism and Possible Use of Viral Diseases," Politics and the Life Sciences, [London], 15, September 1996, 192-93.

This article is a commentary on Jonathan B. Tucker's "Chemical/Biological Terrorism: Coping with a New Threat" (see Tucker, Jonathan B.). Burck identifies the new terrorists as fanatics carrying out the dictates of their moral or philosophical system or revenging perceived high crimes against their group or against groups that the individual fanatic admires. Burck distinguishes three different types of new terrorists: those who seek revolutionary chaos, those who wish to obliterate the structure of society, and those who seek to destroy a racial, ethnic/religious, or social group. He concurs with Tucker's proposal that, rather than identifying attacks, greater global epidemiological intelligence is required to rapidly characterize and pinpoint sources of real public health threats that are the background against which the frenzied features of biological attacks might be more discernible. In addition, he identifies understanding the perceptions, motivations, and intentions of radical groups as another priority.

Keyword(s): biological terrorism; chemical terrorism; biological weapons of mass destruction; chemical weapons of mass destruction; biological agent detection; terrorist cults

Byman, Daniel. "The Logic of Ethnic Terrorism," Studies in Conflict and Terrorism, [London], 21, No. 2, April-June 1998, 149-69.

Ethnic terrorism differs considerably from violence carried out for ideological, religious, or financial motives. Ethnic terrorists often seek to influence their own constituencies more than the country as a whole. Ethnic terrorists frequently seek to foster communal identity, in contrast to an identity proposed by the state. Ethnic terrorists often target potential intermediaries, who might otherwise compromise on identity issues. A secondary goal of the terrorist attacks is to create a climate of fear among a rival group's population. Ethnic terrorism creates a difficult problem for the state: conventional countermeasures may engender broader support for an insurgency or a separatist movement even when they hamstring or defeat a specific terrorist group. Because such strategies often backfire, an ideal strategy is to compel "in-group" policing--encouraging ethnic moderates through carrots as well as sticks to punish radical activity.

Keyword(s): terrorism; counterterrorism; combating terrorism

Campbell, James K. "Excerpts from Research Study "Weapons of Mass Destruction and Terrorism: Proliferation by Non-State Actors"," Terrorism and Political Violence, [London], 9, No. 2, Summer 1997, 24-50.

In the wake of the Cold War, a new world disorder seems to be emerging wherein the legitimacy of many states is being challenged from within by increasing nonstate calls for self-determination from the likes of religious cults, hate groups, isolationist movements, ethnic groups, and revivalist movements. These movements often prey on the insecurities of the population, offering to fill psychological, sociological, political, or religious security needs of those who would join them. Religious-oriented groups appear to share a common ideological thread that rejects existing social, economic, and political structures and demands a structural revision of the world to allow them to become the authoritarian dominant influence. Emanating from these movements will be the "Post-Modern Terrorists," who possess a "ripeness" to threaten use of weapons of mass destruction (CBRNC). This article argues that the terrorist CBRNC threat will emanate from nonstate groups operating under a veneer of religion and ethnic-racist hate. These groups, plus the occasional cult, are the most likely candidates to threaten use of weapons of mass destruction in a mass casualty-causing "super-terrorist act."

Keyword(s): CBRNC; terrorism; terrorist cults

Campbell, James. Weapons of Mass Destruction Terrorism. Seminole, Florida: Interpact Press, 1997.

In a series of thoughtful case studies, the author makes a powerful case that the threat of weapons of mass destruction (CBRNC) terrorism, though still not a high probability, has become significantly greater as a result of recent developments in the fields of weapons proliferation and terrorism. Using examples such as the Japanese police failure to recognize the threat posed by the Aum Shinrikyo cult because of its status as an officially recognized religious group, the author clearly identifies the requirements for security agencies and emergency services to be better prepared for CBRNC terrorism. Any country's capacity to prevent such attacks or to cope with them if they occur is dependent on at least four factors: well-resourced and effective counterterrorism intelligence, including experts in CBRNC technology and proliferation; well-trained and -equipped forces to preempt such threats; well-trained and -equipped emergency-response units; and much better education of political leaders and officials and the general public about the nature of the threat.

Keyword(s): CBRNC; terrorist cults; combating terrorism; counterterrorism; terrorism

Carr, Caleb. "Terrorism as Warfare: The Lessons of Military History," World Policy Journal, 13, Winter 1996-97, 1-12.

The article analyzes the behavior patterns of terrorist individuals and organization using examples from history, attempting to establish where such activity fits among categories of behavior. The relationship of terrorist actions with criminal behavior and with orthodox military behavior is the center of the discussion.

Keyword(s): terrorism (general); antiterrorism; terrorist groups and activities

Carter, Ashton, John Deutch, and Philip Zelikow. "Catastrophic Terrorism: Tackling the New Danger," Foreign Affairs, 77, No. 6, November/December 1998, 80-94.

Although the United States takes conventional terrorism seriously, it is not yet prepared for the new threat of catastrophic terrorism. The authors argue that the U.S. government must create unglamourous but effective systems for accountable decision-making that combine civil, military, and intelligence expertise throughout the chain of command; integrate planning and operational activity; build up institutional capacities; and highlight defensive needs before an incident involving weapons of mass destruction (CBRNC) happens. This strategy has four elements: intelligence and warning, prevention and deterrence, crisis and consequence and warning, prevention and deterrence, crisis and consequence management, and coordinated acquisition of equipment and technology.

Keyword(s): CBRNC; terrorism; antiterrorism; counterterrorism; combating terrorism

Carus, Seth. Bioterrorism, Biocrimes, and Bioassassination. Washington, D.C.: Counterproliferation Research, National Defense University, August 4, 1997.
This report provides a survey of incidents involving the use of biological agents by terrorists, criminals, and assassins. It briefly summarizes each case, highlighting how the agent was used or how it was going to be used. It is limited to cases discussed in open-source literature.

Keyword(s): technology; CBRNC; biological weapons of mass destruction; biological attacks; biological terrorism; chemical, biological, nuclear agents; terrorism (general)

Carus, W. Seth. "The Threat of Bioterrorism," <u>National Defense University Strategic Forum</u>, No. 127, September 1997, entire issue.

The article reviews the history of the use of biological weapons for terrorism. It evaluates the past and present threats, then lays out changes foreseen in availability and international conditions that make the use of biological terrorism more likely in the future

Keyword(s): biological terrorism; terrorism (general); future trends

Cascio, Pat, and John McSweeney. <u>SWAT Battle Tactics</u>. Boulder, CO: Paladin Press, 1996. [Call Number: HV8080.S64C37 1996]

The book describes the equipment, training, and strategy needed in developing an effective SWAT team. Specific recommendations are made in chapters on manpower selection, training, handguns, chemical weapons, hostage negotiations, bomb incidents, clearing buildings, hand-to-hand combat, and infantry tactics.

Keyword(s): technology; counterterrorism; weapons technology; first responders; ad hoc terrorism

Chadwick, Elizabeth. "Terrorism and the Law: Historical Contexts, Contemporary Dilemmas, and the End(s) of Democracy," <u>Crime, Law and Social Change</u>, [Dordrecht], 26, No. 4, 1997, 329-50.

This article explores the outlawing of terrorist acts of political violence in relation to the security interests cited in recent proposals by the Group of Seven (G7) industrialized nations and Russia. These proposals do not define what is prohibited. Instead, they communicate a threat that allows greater attention to be paid officially to "camouflage" charities and terrorist use of the Internet. However, individual perceptions of personal and societal threat are heightened unnecessarily by a constant stream of governmental antiterrorist rhetoric, and by fear of potential abuses in official and unofficial methods of antiterrorist surveillance.

Keyword(s): terrorism; surveillance; cyberterrorism; antiterrorism

Chadwick, Elizabeth. "Terrorism and the Law: Historical Contexts, Contemporary Dilemmas, and the End(s) of Democracy," Crime, Law and Social Change, 26, No. 4, 1996/97, 329-50.

Recent proposals by the Group of 7 (G7) to clamp down on "terrorists" and "terrorism" do not define that which is prohibited. Instead, a threat is communicated that in turn allows, among other things, greater attention to be paid officially to "camouflage" charities and "terrorist" use of the Internet. Nevertheless, it is somewhat of a truism to note that terrorist violence is ultimately defined or characterized, for purposes of legal prohibition, within a highly politicized atmosphere. Starting with a short summary of "antiterrorist" codification efforts made in this century, this article examines some of the "security interests" cited by governments today in their respective struggles against "terrorism." More specifically, it is argued that individual perceptions of personal and societal threat are heightened unnecessarily not only by a constant stream of governmental "antiterrorist" rhetoric, but further, by an awareness of official and unofficial methods of "antiterrorist" surveillance, and the use to which the information so obtained can be put.

Keyword(s): terrorism; antiterrorism; combating terrorism


Chevrier, Marie Isabelle. "The Aftermath of Aum Shinrikyo: A New Paradigm for Terror?," Politics and the Life Sciences, [London], 15, September 1996, 194-96.


The article is a commentary on Jonathan B. Tucker's "Chemical/Biological Terrorism: Coping with a New Threat" (see Tucker, Jonathan B.). Chevrier contends that Tucker's argument has a number of disturbing aspects. She asserts that nearly all definitions of terrorism include political motivation as an essential characteristic. In addition, she argues that Tucker's distinctions between politically motivated terrorists and other more dangerous ones seems strained. Furthermore, Chevrier maintains that Tucker's assertion that religious or racist fanatics are not subject to rational constraints on the scope of their violent acts is an admission of defeat prior to any effort to analyze such organizations and the rational constraints to which they respond.

Keyword(s): biological terrorism; chemical terrorism; chemical weapons of mass destruction; biological weapons of mass destruction; chemical/biological attacks; terrorist cults


Cimbala, Stephen J. "Armies, States, and Terrorism," Strategic Review, 26, Winter 1998, 46-53.

This article addresses challenges of the post-Cold War world, focusing on increased demand for peace operations, the move away from territorial nation states, and visibility of terrorism in an age of media saturation and political disorder. Topics discussed also include operations other than war (OOTW), Russian military interventions, the U.S. role in state-less politics, and why terrorism works.

Keyword(s): terrorism; antiterrorism; combating terrorism

Clark, M.A. "The Pathology of Terrorism: Acts of Violence Directed Against Citizens of the United States while Abroad," Clinical Laboratory Medicine, 18, No. 1, March 1998, 99-114.

Acts of terrorism resulting in serious injury and death have become a daily occurrence in the late 1990s. Forensic pathologists play a key role in the investigation and eventual prosecution of such cases. Meticulous attention to injuries as well as photographic documentation of findings along with the recognition and recovery of trace evidence are critical parts of the autopsy on the victims of terrorist violence. Specific cases of terrorist events from the 1985-97 period are presented along with a detailed explanation of explosion-related injuries.

Keyword(s): improvised explosive device threat or analysis; terrorism; combating terrorism; antiterrorism

Coale, John C. "Fighting Cybercrime," Military Review, 88, No. 2, March-April 1998, 77-82.

The author argues that because of their increasing use and dependence on information technology (IT), the United States and its military are extremely vulnerable to information warfare (IW). The article discusses IW terminology, defensive strategies, statistical failures in IW, and other aspects of IW. The author notes that encryption is a double-edged sword because it gives terrorists and criminals a powerful tool for evading law enforcement.

Keyword(s): technology; antiterrorism; counterterrorism; combating terrorism; information assurance; future trends; information warfare; cyberterrorism

Coates, Joseph F. "A Thriving Future for Terrorism," Technological Forecasting and Social Change, 51, No. 3, 1996, 295-99.

This article defines terrorism as a kind of action undertaken not as a tactic but as a strategic instrument to fulfill some political goal. Governments have only three options available for combating terrorism: to acquiesce to the terrorist's demands, to reach some sort of compromise, and to attack the terrorist group. It is argued that the same elements that are propelling the world toward a global village, such as low-cost telecommunications and transportation, are fueling the conduct of terrorism on a global scale. Further, the three things that compose a significant terrorist threat--compelling issues, a group organized around these issues, and the skills necessary to carry out terrorist action--are also prevalent in the new global order. Given this context, it is suggested that very little can be done to prevent terrorism, but prudent measures can be taken to contain and limit its frequency and severity. Included in these actions are education and training of the populace, training of employees of corporations conducting business overseas, and expanded government gathering of intelligence.

Keyword(s): future trends; antiterrorism; counterterrorism; terrorism; combating terrorism

Cohen, David. "Bombing Business: Terrorist Targeting of Financial Institutions," Jane's Intelligence Review, [London], 9, No. 7, July 1997, 330-34.

The article discusses the vulnerabilities of financial institutions to targeting by terrorists, particularly those motivated by religion. The author explains that financial institutions provide prime targets for religiously motivated groups, whose aim is to destroy the enemy society. For example, the author notes that the targeting of the World Trade Center in 1993, in addition to having significant financial ramifications, was an attempt to destroy a symbol of Western society. He concludes that financial targets will become the targets not only of symbolic attacks but ones carried out with the aim of causing financial chaos.

Keyword(s): antiterrorism; future trends; combating terrorism; infrastructure protection

Cole, Leonard A. "Countering Chem-Bio Terrorism: Limited Possibilities," Politics and the Life Sciences, [London], 15, September 1996, 196-98.

This article is a commentary on Jonathan B. Tucker's "Chemical/Biological Terrorism: Coping with a New Threat" (see Tucker, Jonathan B.). Leonard A. Cole asserts that of the 14 proposals that Tucker offers to address the threat of chemical/biological terrorism, the suggestions for prevention are particularly appealing, but the civil defense recommendations are less credible. In addition, Cole argues that Tucker's proposition for enhanced detection systems is questionable. Cole also considers some of Tucker's detection and response proposals, which he considers to be quite practical.

Keyword(s): biological terrorism; chemical terrorism; CBRNC; biological agent detection; biological decontamination; combating terrorism; counterterrorism

Crenshaw, Martha, and John Pimlott, eds. Encyclopedia of World Terrorism. Armonk, New York: Sharpe Reference, 1997. [Call Number: HV6431 E53 1997]

The first volume of this set introduces the historical background, beginning with an article about the difficulty of defining terrorism. The book largely examines the historical evolution of terrorism and then concludes with a discussion of the different types and techniques of and motivations for terrorism. The second volume concentrates on groups and terrorist activities in the Middle East, Latin America, and post-colonial Asia and Africa (the Palestine Liberation Organization, Tamil Tigers, the massacre at Mai Lai, and so forth). The third volume looks at the problem in the developed world (Irish Republican Army, Earth First, Red Brigades, and so forth) up to the Oklahoma City bombing. It also discusses worldwide ReActions to terrorism. It includes a bibliography and indexes.

Keyword(s): ad hoc and transient terrorist groups; antiterrorism; combating terrorism; terrorism (general); terrorist groups and activities; terrorist cults

Croddy, Eric. Chemical and Biological Warfare: An Annotated Bibliography. Lanham, Maryland, and London: Scarecrow Press, Inc., 1997. [Call Number: Z6724.C5 C76 1997]

The author provides the layman and expert alike with a comprehensive listing of accessible references to chemical and biological weapons. These sources include government documents, World Wide Web sites, research reports, and open media. The introduction assesses the past, present, and future of chemical and biological weapons, especially the role they might play in the hands of terrorists. The book contains more than 2,000 entries and provides excellent citations and abstracts of numerous publications and articles.

Keyword(s): CBRNC; chemical weapons of mass destruction; biological weapons of mass destruction

Croddy, Eric. "Putting the Lid Back on the Chemical Box," Jane's Intelligence Review, [London], 10, No. 1, January 1998, 41-45.

The article discusses the usefulness of the 1993 Chemical Weapons Convention (CWC), which aims to rid the world of chemical weapons (CWs) and their precursors by 2007, while also preemptively controlling the export of CW technologies. Some notable signatories, particularly Russia, have not ratified the document, and other known CW proliferants, such as North Korea, have refused to sign at all. The article postulates four inherent restraints that come into play when trying to anticipate the use of chemical and biological warfare: political backlash, difficulty of manufacturing chemical and biological agents, the extremely high risk factor in storing and handling, and the number of people killed is less important to terrorists than using violence as a political statement. Nevertheless, terrorists added sodium cyanide to the bomb used in the 1993 World Trade Center bombing. The author recommends that nations equip their emergency services for the inevitability of a massive explosion in an urban area, or even chemical and biological warfare weapons used in a future terrorist attack. The article provides a comprehensive listing of CW precursors.

Keyword(s): technology; chemical terrorism; chemical weapons of mass destruction; CBRNC

Davis, Winston. "Dealing with Criminal Religions: The Case of Om Supreme Truth," Christian Century, 112, July 19-26, 1995, 708-11.

The article examines the Japanese Aum Shinrikyo, which released the chemical sarin in the Tokyo subway in 1995, as a religious group and a criminal organization. In the tension between religious freedom and public security, the author concludes, religious tolerance cannot protect cults that are likely to mount such attacks. The Japanese lesson is applied to United States policy.

Keyword(s): terrorist groups and activities; terrorist cults; future trends; chemical terrorism; antiterrorism

Denning, Dorothy E., and William E. Baugh, Jr. Encryption and Evolving Technologies: Tools of Organized Crime and Terrorism. Washington, DC: National Strategy Information Center, 1997.

This essay asserts that access by criminals and terrorists to unbreakable encryption programs poses a serious potential threat to global security. There have already been instances of organized criminals exploiting encryption in Europe and Latin America. The use of communications equipment enhanced by encryption is being used to slow investigations, drive up costs, and deny evidence essential to obtain convictions. Given the need for a secure global information infrastructure, effective policy will require international cooperation. The European Commission and the Organisation for Economic Cooperation and Development are already at work on guidelines.

Keyword(s): technology; information assurance; information warfare; information operations; cyberterrorism


Deutch, John M. "Terrorism," <u>Foreign Policy</u>, No. 108, Fall 1997, 10-22.

The author, a former director of the Central Intelligence Agency (CIA), discusses various new aspects of terrorism. First, terrorists are increasingly operating on an international level rather than in only one region or country. Second, the possibility that terrorists might start using weapons of mass destruction is increasing. Third, cyberterrorists could both divert funds electronically from banks and wreak havoc with a country's air traffic or power-plant control systems. As the terrorist threat increases, countries have to recalibrate the balance between protection of personal liberties and the state's understandable interest in monitoring what is taking place within high-risk foreign-resident communities. The author argues the need for more defensive and offensive countermeasures, particularly by the United States. He also argues for new mechanisms of cooperation both nationally and internationally between intelligence and law-enforcement agencies.

Keyword(s): terrorism; cyberterrorism; CBRNC; counterterrorism; combating terrorism


Deva, Major General Yashwant. "Threats to Cyber Security in the Wake of Pokhran II," <u>Indian Defence Review</u>, [New Delhi], 13, No. 2, April-June 1998, 47-53.

The article discusses cyber security in relation to India's nuclear program, citing as an example a cyber break-in of the Bhabha Atomic Research Centre (BARC) by a hacker. The article examines the nature of cyber security threats, malicious e-mail programs, hacker tools and tricks, and protecting sensitive data. It concludes that a system's reliability involves not only its holes but also its ability to detect its own corruption.

Keyword(s): technology; cyberterrorism; information assurance; combating terrorism; antiterrorism


Drake, C.J.M.. <u>Terrorists' Target Selection</u>. London and New York: Macmillan and St. Martin's, 1998.

The book examines typologies, ideology, strategy, tactics, and capabilities of violent terrorist organizations, and the effect of security and counterterrorist measures. It argues that seemingly irrational violence is frequently the result of a process that is explicable and logical.

Keyword(s): terrorism; terrorist groups and activities; antiterrorism; counterterrorism; combating terrorism

Economist. "Choke Hold," The Economist, [London], 338, February 10, 1996, 79-81.

The article points out that chemical weapons offer devastating power to a technologically astute terrorist. It discusses the risk of terrorists stealing chemical agents from existing stockpiles or developing their own. It also examines the situation in the United States and Russia and international countermeasures, including the 1993 Chemical Weapons Convention. Keeping chemical weapons out of the wrong hands will take law, skill, and luck.

Keyword(s): chemical terrorism; technology; combating terrorism; CBRNC; chemical weapons of mass destruction; chemical attacks


Economist. "The New Terrorism: Coming Soon to a City Near You," The Economist, [London], 348:8081, August 15, 1998, 17-19.

The article suggests that the bombings of the U.S. embassies in Kenya and Tanzania may well form part of a new, even more frightening type of terrorism. A terrorist attack in a shopping mall using anthrax, for example, is one of the scenarios discussed by experts at a conference on biological terrorism held near Washington, DC. According to Bruce Hoffman, the hallmarks of the new terror include "amorphous religious and millenarian aims" and "vehemently anti-government forms of populism, reflecting far-fetched conspiracy notions." New terrorism has no explicit agenda, and its perpetrators have no realistic program for taking power themselves. The target of the new terror is likely to be the United States.

Keyword(s): CBRNC; biological terrorism; biological weapons of mass destruction


Eifried, Gary. "On Countering the Threat of Chemical and Biological Terrorism," Politics and the Life Sciences, [London], 15, September 1996, 199-201.

This article is a commentary on Jonathan B. Tucker's "Chemical/Biological Terrorism: Coping with a New Threat" (see Tucker, Jonathan B.). Tucker focuses on actions at the local and national levels, but greater effort and cooperation at the international level need to be considered. Gary Eifried considers the need to initiate projects to develop chemical warfare terrorism data, to limit access to potential chemical or biological materials and information, to create a virtual response network for exchange of information and ideas as well as a source of data, to establish international response teams, to raise awareness and sensitivity, to reinforce arms control, to expand international law enforcement, to pursue research and development, to set forensic protocols, and to assure recovery capability following a terrorist attack.

Keyword(s): CBRNC; biological terrorism; chemical terrorism; combating terrorism; counterterrorism; biological decontamination; chemical decontamination

Ellenbogen, Mike. "Checking in with New Bomb Detection Strategies," Security Management, 40, No. 2, February 1996, 29-32.

Airlines and regulators are struggling with how best to protect passengers from the threat of terrorist attempts to plant explosives. Detecting explosives is more difficult than detecting weapons, because explosives are not metallic and do not appear in predictable shapes. Progress is being made, however. Several promising technologies are being developed. The article discusses the distinctly different approaches to the problem being taken by the United States and Europe.

Keyword(s): technology; aviation security; inspection of aircraft cargo containers; inspection of carry-on luggage; inspection of aircraft passengers; antiterrorism; combating terrorism


Epstein, Jeffrey H. "The Risk of Nuclear Terrorism," The Futurist, 32, No. 4, May 1998, 10.

Law-enforcement agencies planning to combat the threat of terrorism are growing ever-more anxious about the prospect of nuclear weapons being used by terrorists. Although it still represents a low risk, this possibility has increased dramatically in the last few years, says Brian Jenkins, a former RAND researcher and a top expert in international terrorism. Jenkins believes, however, that terrorists have little incentive to use nuclear weapons given the devastation that can be caused with conventional bombs.

Keyword(s): nuclear terrorism; CBRNC; weapons of mass destruction in urban areas


Falkenrath, Richard A. "Chemical/Biological Terrorism: Coping with Uncertain Threats and Certain Vulnerabilities," Politics and the Life Sciences, [London], 15, September 1996, 201-2.

This article is a commentary on Jonathan B. Tucker's "Chemical/Biological Terrorism: Coping with a New Threat" (see Tucker, Jonathan B.). Tucker's article provides a valuable contribution to the literature on weapons of mass destruction in its well-conceived prescriptive agenda, but his argument, according to Richard A. Falkenrath, could be enhanced in three ways. First, Tucker specifies the conditions under which a terrorist group might employ chemical/biological (C/B) weapons with disproportionate precision and confidence given the lack of hard data. Second, Tucker's argument for a more focused U.S. response to C/B terrorism could be reinforced by sharply differentiating the C/B threat from the C/B vulnerability. Finally, the paper would benefit from an investigation of the bureaucratic barriers to the implementation of his policy agenda.

Keyword(s): CBRNC; chemical terrorism; biological terrorism; combating terrorism; counterterrorism; biological weapons of mass destruction; chemical weapons of mass destruction


Forrow, L., and V.W. Sidel. "Medicine and Nuclear War," JAMA [Journal of the American Medical Association], No. 280, August 5, 1998, 456-60.

To determine how physicians might participate in the prevention of nuclear war in the post-Cold War era, the authors review, from a medical perspective, the history of the nuclear weapons era since Hiroshima and the status of today's nuclear arsenals and dangers. Today's dangers include nuclear arms proliferation, an increasing risk of nuclear terrorism, and the 35,000 warheads that remain in superpower nuclear arsenals.

Keyword(s): nuclear terrorism; CBRNC; first responders; antiterrorism; combating terrorism; nuclear weapons of mass destruction

Forster, Anthony. "An Emerging Threat Shapes Up as Terrorists Take to the High Seas," Jane's Intelligence Review, 10, No. 7, July 1998, 42-45.

Increasingly, maritime violence is constituting more than mere piracy, as more and more militant groups seek to further their political aims offshore. The author charts this emerging trend and examines how the threat can be countered. By examining the current threat environment, he helps to explain how navies and security forces of the world can be better prepared for naval terrorism, and how they can prevent naval terrorist attacks before they occur. He notes that one of the most active threats is Egypt's Gama'a al-Islamiya, a radical Muslim group. Other active groups are the Liberation Tigers of Tamil Eelam (LTTE), the Moro Islamic Liberation Front, and the Armed Islamic Group (GIA). The seminal event in modern maritime terrorism was, however, the hijacking of the "Achille Lauro" by Palestine Liberation Front terrorists on October 7, 1985.

Keyword(s): terrorism (general); antiterrorism; future trends; counterterrorism; combating terrorism

Freundlich, Naomi. "Countering the Poor Man's Nuclear Weapons," Business Week, No. 3506, December 16, 1996, 128-30.

Biological weapons were banned by the United Nations (UN) in 1972, but they are spreading. Recent intelligence reports suggest that 17 countries might be developing biological weapons, including Iraq, Iran, Syria, China, and North Korea. Experts are also worried about the spread of the weapons to terrorist groups. The appeal of biological agents is that they are cheap and powerful. Although the threat of biological weapons has grown, research on detection devices, protective suits, and antidotes to germ agents has lagged.

Keyword(s): technology; CBRNC; biological weapons of mass destruction; biological terrorism; antiterrorism; combating terrorism; biological agent detection

Fulghum, David A. "Secrecy About Raids Hints at More to Come," Aviation Week and Space Technology, 149, No. 9, August 31, 1998, 30-32.

The deepening silence out of the Pentagon about the details of the raids on Afghanistan and Sudan and the limited nature of these two strikes are signs that there are additional raids planned against other sites associated with terrorists, say Pentagon officials, defense specialists, and former military leaders. The United States fired 79 cruise missiles at seven targets--a pharmaceutical plant in Khartoum, Sudan, and up to six training, support, and headquarters areas south of Kabul, Afghanistan, said officials.

Keyword(s): combating terrorism; counterterrorism; antiterrorism

Gee, John. "CBW Terrorism and the Chemical Weapons Convention," Politics and the Life Sciences, [London], 15, September 1996, 203-4.

This article is a commentary on Jonathan B. Tucker's "Chemical/Biological Terrorism: Coping with a New Threat" (see Tucker, Jonathan B.). Tucker's analysis supports the view that it was mainly the choice of the weapon for the target and difficulties in producing and handling chemical weapons (CW) that resulted in CW's low rate of use as weapons of terror until now. Tucker reveals that the chemical attacks orchestrated by Aum Shinrikyo in Japan in 1994 and 1995 removed the old psychological barrier that inhibited the use of CW by terrorists, with the move to indiscriminate killing being the desired result of a terrorist assault. This move makes the threat of chemical/biological terrorism more real. John Gee considers Tucker's view on the constraints related to any bid to produce or otherwise to attain such weapons in the absence of a state weapons program and offers some views on the possible role of the Chemical Weapons Convention in tackling the issue at a national and international level.

Keyword(s): chemical weapons of mass destruction; chemical terrorism; combating terrorism; counterterrorism

Geissler, Erhard. "Joint International Action Is Necessary to Counter the Threat of Chemical/Biological Terrorism," Politics and the Life Sciences, [London], 15, September 1996, 205-7.

This article is a commentary on Jonathan B. Tucker's "Chemical/Biological Terrorism: Coping with a New Threat" (see Tucker, Jonathan B.). Erhard Geissler is convinced by Tucker's well-founded argument that the chemical/biological terrorist threat is now real, but he questions the possibilities of using molecular biotechnology to optimize biological and toxin warfare agents. Geissler challenges Tucker's definition of biological warfare and toxin warfare agents and the possibilities for delivering them.

Keyword(s): CBRNC; chemical terrorism; biological terrorism; chemical weapons of mass destruction; biological weapons of mass destruction; combating terrorism; counterterrorism

Gips, Michael A. "Hot Spots Around the World," Security Management, 42, No. 5, 1998, 79-82.

At the Department of State's annual Government/Industry Conference on Terrorism, held in Washington, D.C., members of the Office of Intelligence and Threat Analysis presented country risk analyses for Asia, the Former Soviet Union (FSU), and Europe. East Asia is said to be the safest region in the world, but dangerous areas within the region exist. As a whole, crime is more common than terrorism in East Asia and the Pacific. In the South Asian region, which includes India, Pakistan, Sri Lanka, and Afghanistan, terrorism continues to be a major concern. Terrorist groups in Europe have been categorized into separatist groups and Marxist-Leninist groups. The latter have been reduced from ten to two. The decline is attributed to cooperation between European governments and the fact that "Marxism-Leninism is a harder sell nowadays." The article discusses in detail the risk analyses for each country in Asia and Europe.

Keyword(s): terrorism; terrorist groups and activities; antiterrorism; combating terrorism


Gips, Michael. "Bioterrorism in Our Midst?," Security Management, 41, No. 11, November 1997, 12.

At the Conference on Countering Biological Terrorism: Strategic Firepower in the Hands of Many?, held by the Potomac Institute for Policy Studies, two types of groups were identified as posing the highest threat of biological attack: religious fundamentalist terrorists and right-wing fanatics.

Keyword(s): CBRNC; biological weapons of mass destruction; antiterrorism; combating terrorism; biological terrorism


Gotowicki, Stephen H. "Confronting Terrorism: New War Form or Mission Impossible?," Military Review, 87, No. 3, May-June 1997, 61-66.

The author, a lieutenant colonel in the U.S. Army, argues that terrorism, rather than a military problem, is a political, social, and economic problem. The military, by its nature, is not suitably structured, trained, or equipped to defeat terrorism. The author believes that, although the military may be able to contribute to the fight against terrorism, it should not lead the fight.

Keyword(s): combating terrorism; counterterrorism; future trends; antiterrorism


Grosscup, Beau. The Newest Explosions of Terrorism: Latest Sites of Terrorism in the 1990s and Beyond. New Horizon Press, 1998.

This book challenges conventional understandings as they developed over the past decades and offers a new framework to assess internal and international terrorism in the new millennium. Topics include historical foundations, antiterrorist mobilization, U.S. foreign policy, Northern Ireland and Britain, Germany, Sri Lanka and India, and the Middle East.

Keyword(s): terrorism; terrorist groups and activities


Guelke, Adrian. "Wars of Fear: Coming to Grips with Terrorism," Harvard International Review, 20, No. 4, Fall 1998, 44-47.

In August 1998, a series of events prompted a new wave of concern about terrorism. The bombings of the U.S. embassies in Kenya and Tanzania killed hundreds of people; the most deadly attack in the thirty-year conflict in Northern Ireland took place in the town of Omagh; and a pipebomb exploded at a Planet Hollywood restaurant in Cape Town, injuring scores of tourists. However, the term "terrorism" is misleading because it implies that certain acts of violence can be treated as a single phenomenon, despite their different origins and the variety of motivations of their perpetrators. Western governments have tended to use the term to demonize any violent group, notwithstanding the different contexts in which violence takes place, and the varying inclinations of perpetrators to jeopardize the lives of innocent bystanders.

Keyword(s): terrorism; antiterrorism; combating terrorism


Hayward, Douglas. "Net-Based Terrorism a Myth," TechWeb, November 19, 1997, 1-2.

The article highlights a statement made by Neil Barrett, a principal security consultant for Groupe Bull, at a seminar on digital terrorism held at the International Centre for Security Analysis in London. According to Barrett, terrorist groups are not using the Internet for anything more than propaganda and internal communications. However, terrorist leaders are aware that the Internet could be used as a conduit for information warfare (IW) attacks aimed at crippling information security (IS) systems crucial to the operation of military and civilian organizations. Barrett explained that reports of Net-based terrorist incidents are based on a misunderstanding of the difference between terrorism and malicious or politically motivated hacking.

Keyword(s): technology; cyberterrorism; information warfare; infrastructure protection


Hayward, Douglas. "Terrorists Target the Net," TechWeb News, May 8, 1998, .

Terrorist groups are looking to launch Net-based attacks on the computer networks of governments and businesses, according to speakers at an international security conference held in Brussels. Some terrorists are already considering how to use the Net to launch "information warfare" attacks against the information technologies (IT) infrastructures of governments, utilities, and businesses. Organizations such as the Irish Republican Army (IRA) have noticed recently that computer systems are often the most important and expensive casualty of bombs placed in commercial areas. This has encouraged terrorist groups to consider ways of crippling their enemies' IT capabilities. Evidence of a shift by terrorists toward attacks on economic infrastructure targets is already emerging, according to a second British academic at the conference.

Keyword(s): technology; cyberterrorism; information warfare; combating terrorism; antiterrorism


Henderson, D.A. "Bioterrorism as a Public Health Threat," Emerging Infectious Diseases, 4, No. 3, July-September 1998, [np].

The long ignored and denied threat of bioterrorism has heightened over the past few years. Recent events in Iraq, Japan, and Russia cast an ominous shadow. Two candidate agents are of special concern: smallpox and anthrax. The magnitude of the problems and the gravity of the scenarios associated with release of these organisms have been vividly portrayed by two epidemics of smallpox in Europe during the 1970s and by an accidental release of aerosolized anthrax from a Russian bioweapons facility in 1979. Efforts in the United States to deal with possible incidents involving bioweapons in the civilian sector have only recently begun and have made only limited progress. Only with substantial additional resources at the federal, state, and local levels can a credible and meaningful response be mounted. For longer-term solutions, the medical community must educate both the public and policy makers about bioterrorism and build a global consensus condemning its use.

Keyword(s): CBRNC; biological weapons of mass destruction; biological terrorism; antiterrorism; counterterrorism; combating terrorism

Heylin, Michael. "Technology and the Changing Face of War," Chemical and Engineering News, 76, No. 19, May 11, 1998, 26.

An article in the April 27, 1998, issue of Aviation Week and Space Technology reported on the proceedings of a meeting of national security experts and theoreticians at the Army War College in Carlisle, Pennsylvania. The meeting predicted that conflict in the future will be shaped heavily by the epochal, technology-driven change from the industrial age to the information age that is currently well under way. Wars between nations will likely take a backseat to a range of conflicts that may occur almost anywhere under various guises outside of today's norms of international law and rules of engagement. Amorphous enemies without territories or borders could become a greater danger than traditional nation-state rivalries as "cyberstates" replace nations as the typical adversary.

Keyword(s): technology; cyberterrorism; CBRNC; information assurance; information operations; future trends; information warfare

Heylin, Michael. "The Chemicals of War," Chemical and Engineering News, 76, No. 10, March 9, 1998, 27.

The possibility of a war with Iraq over the United Nations inspections system for chemical and biological weapons (CBWs) and the arrest of two suspects in Las Vegas on charges of possessing a material for use as a biological weapon (anthrax) have placed chemistry and biology in the forefront of national concerns. Today, CBWs are classified with nuclear weapons in a special category--weapons of mass destruction. This classification reflects the option apparently retained by the United States to retaliate with nuclear weapons to a chemical or biological attack on its territory, its forces, or its allies. It is the capacity to produce CBWs that presents a particular dilemma for those striving to contain them. The list of roughly 20 nations that, according to the United States, have CBW capacity, reads like a list of rogue states.

Keyword(s): technology; chemical terrorism; biological terrorism; CBRNC; chemical weapons of mass destruction; combating terrorism; antiterrorism; biological weapons of mass destruction

Hoffman, Bruce. Inside Terrorism. New York: Columbia University Press, 1998. [Call Number: HV6431.H626 1998]

The book places today's terrorist groups and individuals in the context of the history of international terrorism. The author identifies a change in motivation and strategy that is attributed to the increasing predominance of religious over political terrorism. The analysis of the former mind set shows a greater propensity for violence, which the author explores.

Keyword(s): future trends; antiterrorism; chemical/biological attacks; terrorist groups and activities

Hoffman, Bruce. ""Holy Terror": The Implications of Terror Motivated by a Religious Imperative," Studies in Conflict and Terrorism, 19, October-December 1995, 271-84.

The article explores the origins of the connection between religious beliefs and terrorist activity, together with their linkage in the upsurge of religion-connected terrorism in the last fifteen years. The author notes that the Middle East is not the only area where this is happening, noting that extremists in the United States are legitimizing terrorist acts by religious beliefs and goals.

Keyword(s): terrorist groups and activities; terrorism (general); terrorist cults

Hoffman, Bruce. "The Confluence of International and Domestic Trends in Terrorism," Terrorism and Political Violence, [London], 9, No. 2, Summer 1997, 1-15.

This article assesses the changing nature of terrorism in the 1990s within the context of the growing overlap between international and domestic terrorist trends and its potential implications for aviation security. It argues that the emergence of either obscure, idiosyncratic millenarian movements or zealously nationalist religious groups possibly represent a very different and potentially far more lethal threat than more 'traditional' terrorist adversaries. Further, as these threats are both domestic as well as international, the response must therefore be both national and multinational. In this respect, national cohesiveness and organizational preparation will necessarily remain the essential foundation for building the effective multinational approach appropriate to these new threats.

Keyword(s): aviation security; terrorism; antiterrorism; antiterrorism; terrorist cults; counterterrorism

Hogg, Ian V.. Counter-Terrorism Equipment. London: Greenhill Books, 1997. [Call Number: HV8080.S64H64 1997]

The book describes and pictures a wide range of current equipment--weapons, surveillance equipment, vehicles, bomb disposal and detection devices, and protective materials and clothing--used in counterterrorist operations of various types. Presented as a sampling of technology now in use, the book provides one-page summaries of the operating characteristics and functions of the items displayed, with identification of country of origin (US, European, Israeli, and South African).

Keyword(s): technology; counterterrorism; weapons technology; future trends

Hoo, Kevin Soo, Seymour Goodman, and Lawrence Greenberg. "Information Technology and the Terrorist Threat," Survival: The IISS Quarterly, [London], 39, No. 3, Autumn 1997, 135-55.

In recent years, developed countries have embraced the information technologies (IT) of digital computing and telecommunications, extensively integrating them into their militaries, economies, and societies. This new trend has greatly increased the vulnerability of the new information infrastructure to criminals, terrorists, competing companies, foreign intelligence officers, foreign military personnel, and hackers. Each group has its own characteristics and capabilities. This article examines how IT might be used to enable or enhance terrorist activities. It begins with a brief look at the defining features, tactics, and motives of modern terrorism. It then analyzes how the diffusion of IT might affect terrorist practice and practitioners. It concludes with some tentative thoughts on how current governmental responses to terrorism might be extended to deal with IT-enabled terrorism.

Keyword(s): technology; cyberterrorism; combating terrorism; counterterrorism; antiterrorism; information assurance; terrorism

Howard, Colonel Bruce K. "From Sandbags to Computers: What's New in Field Fortifications and Protective Structures," Engineer: The Professional Bulletin for Army Engineers, 27, April 1997, 28-31.

New materials and methods provide vastly better protection, with significantly less manpower, for soldiers and their equipment and supplies. The article discusses various new protection methods, including a Windows-based software program that helps engineers predict and prioritize the resources required for various levels of survivability and to design roof support structures and determine the depth of soil needed to cover the structure, based on the threat weapon. It notes that the U.S. Army Engineer Waterways Experiment Station (WES) is developing an Antiterrorism (AT) Planner to help engineer officers plan and implement optimum protective measures. The author notes that additional information on these and other WES research and development projects can be found at the Worldwide Web site http://www.wes.army mil.

Keyword(s): technology; antiterrorism; blast mitigation; combating terrorism; building collapse

Ismail, Jamal. "'I am not afraid of death': Osama bin Laden Talks About the Embassy Bombings, the Strikes on Iraq and his War on America," Newsweek, January 11, 1999, 36-37.

This article is an interview by Palestinian journalist Jamal Ismail with Osama bin Laden, conducted deep in Afghan mountain ranges controlled by the Taliban. Bin Laden, the alleged international terrorist, discusses the bombings of U.S. embassies in Africa, the U.S. military attack on Iraq, and the bounty on his head. He states: "We don't consider it a crime if we tried to have nuclear, chemical, biological weapons."

Keyword(s): terrorism; terrorist groups and activities; CBRNC

Jacobs, G. "Information War in the Future." Pages 113-20 in SP'S Military Yearbook. ed. Jayant Baranwal. [New Delhi], Guide Publications, 1997. [Call Number: U10.I5 M5]

The author discusses the role of on-line data systems in warfare of the late 20th century and thereafter. In the future, an increasingly important part of warfare will be "information war" or "cyberwar" in which opponents will seek to disable or disrupt electronic communication and data control systems. Such attacks could entail direct military assault, the activities of computer "hackers," or terrorists. The author discusses the nature of "the information war" and the various steps the U.S. military is taking to wage it and to protect itself against it. lb

Keyword(s): technology; cyberterrorism; future trends; assurance/warfare/operations

Jacquard, Roland, and Dominique Nasplezes. Carlos: Le Dossier secret. Paris: Jean Picollec, 1997 [in French]. [Call Number: HV6431 .J317 1997]

This book traces the career of Illich Ramirez-Sanchez, also known as Carlos the Jackal. It discusses terrorist acts that he committed in France and other European countries during the 1971-77 period, efforts to find him during 1978-92, and his arrest by French authorities in Khartoum, Sudan, in August 1994. The account is based on confidential police files.

Keyword(s): terrorism; terrorist groups and activities; counterterrorism; combating terrorism

Johnson, Larry C. "The Fall of Terrorism," Security Management, 41, No. 4, April 1997, 26-32.

In the author's view, terrorism data of the Central Intelligence Agency (CIA) and Federal Bureau of Investigation (FBI) reveal the danger as more fear than fact. If the purpose of terrorism is to reach beyond its immediate victims and engender fear in the collective psyche, then an important part of any government's countermeasure strategy should be to keep the reality of terrorist activity in perspective. Unfortunately, that battle is not being fought, much less won. Public fears and government comments notwithstanding, terrorism is not on the rise. Raw statistics demonstrate that the level of terrorist violence has declined since the mid-1980s. International and domestic terrorist incidents are approaching historic lows. Terrorism is down for several reasons: sound government policy, aggressive law enforcement, and the breakup of the Soviet Union.

Keyword(s): terrorism (general); combating terrorism; counterterrorism; antiterrorism

Juergensmeyer, Mark. "Terror Mandated by God," Terrorism and Political Violence, [London], 9, No. 2, Summer 1997, 16-23.

Religion's renewed presence on a global scale is often accompanied by violence for three reasons in particular: the nature of religion and its claims for power over life in death; the nature of secular politics, which places its own legitimacy on the currency of weapons and can only be challenged successfully on a military level; and the nature of political violence. The symbolic power of violence can be a valuable commodity for religious as well as for political forces. Through violence, the proponents of a religious ideology like Aum Shinrikyo remind the populace of the godly power that makes their ideology potent, and at times religious activists create man-made incidents of terror on God's behalf.

Keyword(s): terrorist cults; terrorism

Kaplan, David E. "Terrorism's Next Wave: Nerve Gas and Germs," U.S. News and World Report, 123, November 17, 1997, 26.

Federal officials are aware of a new breed of college-educated extremist threatening to use biological, radiological, or chemical weapons to achieve his or her goals. Investigators have discovered biochemical agents in the possession of political extremists, extortionists, murderers, and the mentally ill, and the Federal Bureau of Investigation is currently involved in 50 investigations of individuals suspected of using or planning to use radiological, biological, or chemical agents. Behind all of this is a very real fear that the world has entered a new stage in terrorism. Widespread technical education and high-tech communications have dramatically increased the number of people who know how to synthesize chemicals and culture bacteria. Books and videos on making these substances, and turning them into weapons, can be obtained on the Internet, at gun shows and survivalist fairs, and through the mail.

Keyword(s): technology; chemical terrorism; biological terrorism; CBRNC; biological weapons of mass destruction; cyberterrorism; chemical weapons of mass destruction

Kash, Douglas A.. "An International Legislative Approach to 21st-Century Terrorism." Pages 163-72 in The Future of Terrorism: Violence in the New Millennium. Harvey W. Kushner, ed. Thousand Oaks, CA: Sage Publications, 1998. [Call Number: HV6432.F87 1998]

The author makes a plea for multinational legislative efforts and agreements to combat international terrorism. He reviews international meetings that have sought to define terrorism and to lay the groundwork for international legal measures to control terrorists, without which terrorists otherwise find safe havens in countries without antiterrorist laws or enforcement agencies.

Keyword(s): antiterrorism; combating terrorism

Katzman, Kenneth. Terrorism: National Security Policy and the Home Front. Carlisle Barracks, Pennsylvania: U.S. Army War College, 1995. [Call Number: HV6431.T483 1995]

The chapter gives a detailed sketch of the Hizbollah's position, and goals as a terrorist organization and of the international circumstances likely to influence its further activities. Substantial attention goes to its modes of operation and to possible changes in response to changing conditions, with emphasis on ramifications for US antiterrorist policy.

Keyword(s): terrorist groups and activities; future trends

Kelly, Robert J. "Moral Disengagement and the Role of Ideology in the Displacement and Diffusion of Responsibility among Terrorists," Eurocriminology, [London], 11, 1997, 3-24.

This essay explores the intellectual artifacts and mechanisms that enable terrorists to kill indiscriminately in the name of political, social, or cultural causes. Most terrorist campaigns are methods to establish claims for a notion of justice, to seek new societies, or to release frustration that cannot be satisfactorily ameliorated through normal political channels. Thus, solutions to the problem of terrorism seem invariably beyond the narrow frameworks of counterterrorism. Without an effort to penetrate the political language and self-understanding of terrorist organizations, policies to counteract them or to open up nonviolent alternatives do not seem possible.

Keyword(s): terrorism; counterterrorism; antiterrorism; combating terrorism

Khatchadourian, Haig. The Morality of Terrorism. New York: P. Lang, 1998. [Call Number: HV6431.K4398]

This book argues that terrorism violates certain human rights, just war, and "consequentialist" moral principles, and so is always wrong. In distinguishing "freedom fighting" from terrorism, this study lays down stringent conditions derived from just war theory, for the moral justifiability of "freedom fighting," such as some revolutions, civil wars, and guerrilla warfare. The book then evaluates the morality of actual and possible judicial and military responses to terrorism by targeted governments. An appendix provides a case study (the Palestine problem) of root causes of political and moralistic-religious terrorism.

Keyword(s): antiterrorism; terrorism; combating terrorism; counterterrorism

Killebrew, Kenneth Carroll, Jr. Critical Events and Agenda Building in the United States and Britain: A Comparative Analysis of the Communication Effects of Terrorist Acts on Elite Newspaper Coverage and Policy Statements. University of Tennessee, 1998.

This Ph.D. dissertation examines the relationship between mass media news coverage and policymaking statements through a comparative study of two nations, using two critical events of political violence/terrorism. It attempts to determine the agenda-building nature of these events on the agendas of the news media and government policymakers in the United States and Britain. The research also seeks to determine the nature of the relationship between news coverage and the news organization's proximity to a critical event through content analysis. The critical events studied in the dissertation include the 1992 mortar attack at No. 10 Downing Street by the Irish Republican Army (IRA) and the 1993 bombing of the World Trade Center in New York City.

Keyword(s): terrorism; terrorist groups and activities

Laqueur, Walter. "Postmodern Terrorism," Foreign Affairs, 75, No. 5, September-October, 1996, 24-36.

The article traces changes in world terrorist activities and strategies in recent years, citing numerous examples of diversification and adaptation. The author offers scenarios for future changes, analyzing motivations, available technology, and political conditions that might influence terrorist behavior or even cause it to end.

Keyword(s): future trends; terrorist groups and activities; biological terrorism; chemical terrorism; cyber terrorism; terrorism (general)

Laqueur, Walter. "Terror's New Face: The Radicalization and Escalation of Modern Terrorism," Harvard International Review, 20, No. 4, Fall 1998, 48-51.

The author stresses the need for much rethinking about terrorism because the terrorist acts of the past do not necessarily offer a reliable guide for the future. Only an examination of the changing face of terrorism and an analysis of current trends can offer valuable insights into future outbreaks. Although some terrorists are still patriots and genuine revolutionaries, this pattern is no longer typical. Any survey of the world map of terrorism--the parts of the world where the most casualties take place--would reveal the emergence of other features. The author's survey reveals not only a growing fanaticism but also the growth of indiscriminate murder, the desire to exercise power, and sheer bloodlust.

Keyword(s): terrorism; future trends; terrorist cults

Laqueur, Walter. "Terrorism via the Internet," The Futurist, 31, March-April 1997, 64-5.

Walter Laqueur believes that the Internet could become a new target for terrorists. Writing in Foreign Affairs, Laqueur notes that modern society is becoming increasingly reliant on electronic storage, retrieval, analysis, and transmission of information. This trend offers the new generation of terrorists a highly attractive target. With the potential threat to these online resources, governments and law-enforcement agencies are now taking the concepts of infoterrorism and cyberwarfare more seriously.

Keyword(s): technology; future trends; cyberterrorism; information assurance operations; antiterrorism; counterterrorism; combating terrorism

Leader, Stefan H. "The Rise of Terrorism," Security Management, 41, No. 4, April 1997, 34-39.

The U.S. government's numbers on terrorism would seem to suggest that terrorism is not a rising risk. But the government's statistics present a very limited view of the landscape. In the Department of State's view, an incident is classified as international terrorism only if it involves the citizens or territory of more than one country. Data gathered by Pinkerton Risk Assessment Services are based on a different definition of terrorism and show many more incidents of terrorism worldwide during 1995 than do State Department statistics. Pinkerton's data show more terrorism and political violence in the 1990s, whereas the State Department's data show more in the 1980s. Terrorism confined to one country and the killing or injuring of only its citizens appear to be up. The author explains why the Aum Shinrikyo attack on the Tokyo subway with the sarin nerve agent was a seminal event.

Keyword(s): terrorism (general); antiterrorism; combating terrorism


Leader, Stefan. "Cash for Carnage: Funding the Modern Terrorist," Jane's Intelligence Review, [London], 10, No. 5, May 1998, 42-46.

Noting that terrorists need substantial infusions of cash to finance increasingly complex and costly activities and operations, the article examines sources of terrorist funding, including state sponsorship, private individuals, bank heists and other robberies, kidnaping for ransom, counterfeiting, drug sales, investments and legitimate businesses, other terrorist groups, and cyber crime. The article concludes that terrorist money trails can be followed, but that shutting the money off may prove more difficult with terrorists than with criminals.

Keyword(s): terrorism; combating terrorism; antiterrorism; counterterrorism


Ledeen, Michael. "Terrorism: It Ain't What It Used to Be," International Economics, 9, July-August 1995, 46-47, 68-69.

The article analyzes the similarities and differences between terrorism of the 1990s and that of earlier decades. Given the changes that are identified, current antiterrorism policy is found to be adjusting too slowly, failing to keep up with important new trends.

Keyword(s): future trends; terrorist groups and activities; antiterrorism


Lesce, Tony. "Terrorist Stealth Attack: Chemical/Biological Weapons," S.W.A.T., 16, No. 9, March 1998, 53-57.

State-sponsored chemical and biological weapons (CBW) terrorism is far more likely to occur in the near future than nuclear terrorism. Alternately, groups of terrorists can develop CBW without help from a friendly government. The article discusses the numerous advantages afforded by CBW to terrorists, including the lack of effective countermeasures. It concludes that the United States is very vulnerable to CBW attacks, especially because U.S. security is totally ineffective against CBW agents.

Keyword(s): CBRNC; chemical weapons of mass destruction; biological terrorism; chemical terrorism; combating terrorism; antiterrorism; biological weapons of mass destruction

LeVine, Victor T., and Barbara A. Salent. "Does a Coercive Official Response Deter Terrorism?," Terrorism and Political Violence [London], 8, No. 1, Spring 1996, 22-49.

The article evaluates one type of official response to terrorism, labeled the coercive response. The example cited is the Israeli response to terrorist actions by the Palestine Liberation Organization and the influence of that policy on subsequent overseas terrorist acts.

Keyword(s): terrorist groups and activities; counterterrorism; antiterrorism

Litvin, Stephen W. "Tourism: The World's Peace Industry?," Journal of Travel Research, 37, No. 1, 1998, 63-66.

Tourism is not the creator of peace, but rather, it is one industry that flourishes in the presence of peace. For one, tourism can be successful, or can increase its chances of success, if there is an absence of war, terrorism, and random violence. This means that tourism cannot thrive if there is no peace. Also, the tourism industry is prone to be taken hostage in times of relative peace, resulting in the degeneration of the peace process. For example, terrorists in Egypt concentrated their acts on the country's tourism industry by threatening the safety of tourists, costing Egypt at least US$1 billion in tourism.

Keyword(s): terrorism

Livingstone, Neil C. "Terrorism, Conspiracy, Myth, and Reality," Fletcher Forum of World Affairs, 22, Winter-Spring 1998, 1-15.

The article examines the role of the conservative Right and the liberal Left in the United States in claiming terrorist conspiracies. It focuses on the theory that the former Soviet Union supplied weapons and support for many international terrorists, mainly after 1980. The article includes the role of, and conspiracies regarding, Cuba, Libya's Muammar Qaddafi, Carlos "the Jackal," and Ramzi Yousef in international terrorism.

Keyword(s): terrorism; terrorist groups and activities

Lukasik, S.J., L.T. Greenberg, and S.E. Goodman. "Protecting an Invaluable and Ever-Widening Infrastructure," Communications of the ACM, 41, No. 6, June 1998, 11-16.

The industrial revolution greatly increased the extent and complexity of the world's infrastructure, its connectivity, and its technical and economic interdependencies. Developed nations have, over the past generation, entered a second, equally significant period, that of the information revolution. Concerns about the integrity of modern information technologies (IT)-based infrastructure systems go beyond traditional threats, because even limited failures in extensive and interconnected systems can cause widespread disruption and damage. In addition to hostile nation-states, international and domestic terrorism and organized crime have the demonstrated potential to undermine societies. These emerging concerns over the vulnerabilities of modern infrastructures have been highlighted by the President's Commission on Critical Infrastructure Protection (PCCIP). The PCCIP's report may be viewed as a call for prudent actions.

Keyword(s): cyberterrorism; infrastructure protection; combating terrorism; antiterrorism


MacKenzie, Debora. "Bioarmageddon," New Scientist, [London], 159, No. 2152, September 19, 1998, 42-46.

Experts met in Stockholm, Sweden, in May 1998, to discuss the terrorist threat of biological attack on civilians. The threat that terrorists may someday turn to this form of attack is no longer in doubt, as they would have little trouble in acquiring biological weapons. Novel antibioweapon technologies are needed to limit the devastation and provide civilian defense.

Keyword(s): CBRNC; biological weapons of mass destruction; technology; antiterrorism; counterterrorism; combating terrorism


MacKenzie, Debora. "Bioarmageddon," New Scientist, [London], 159, No. 2152, September 19, 1998, 42-46.

Until recently, biological defense strategies have been designed to protect soldiers on the battlefield. However, terrorism threats are shifting this focus to how to protect ordinary people in cities. Topics discussed include terrorism, biological weapons, and policy making.

Keyword(s): CBRNC; biological weapons of mass destruction; antiterrorism; combating terrorism; biological terrorism


MacKenzie, Debora. "Bioterrorism Special Report: Bioarmageddon," New Scientist, [London], 157, September 19, 1998, 4-7.

Taking as a given that sooner or later there is going to be a biological attack on a major city, the article discusses various scenarios. With bioweapons so readily available, it asks how governments can protect their citizens from a terrorist armed with anthrax, smallpox, or plague. It notes that novel technologies are needed for civilian defense. However, in Europe disease surveillance is only beginning to be organized on the continent-wide scale needed to track a biological emergency. One answer discussed at a Stockholm conference would be for hospitals to have the type of high-tech detectors being developed to identify airborne pathogens on the battlefield. The article also discusses devices based on antibodies, vaccines, and the speed that is needed in responding to a bioterrorist attack.

Keyword(s): technology; CBRNC; biological weapons of mass destruction; biological terrorism; combating terrorism; counterterrorism; antiterrorism

MacKenzie, Debora. "Bioterrorism Special Report: Deadly Secrets," New Scientist, [London], 157, February 28, 1998, 3-7.

The article questions why the United States will not allow random inspections of biotechnology laboratories. Most governments agree that the 1972 Biological and Toxin Weapons Convention (BTWC) is ineffective, because it provides no legal means to check if countries are complying. Although treaty members are now trying to strengthen the convention to include a system of verification, the U.S. government, under pressure from its drugs and biotechnology industries, rejects this idea. Companies fear that such visits would expose trade secrets. The article discusses these double standards and the stalemate in negotiations on the BTWC.

Keyword(s): CBRNC; biological weapons of mass destruction; biological terrorism; combating terrorism; antiterrorism; counterterrorism

Mann, Paul. "Bin Laden Linked to Nuclear Effort," Aviation Week and Space Technology, 149, No. 15, October 12, 1998, 58.

The Federal Bureau of Investigation (FBI) alleges that a close associate of Osama bin Laden, the affluent Saudi exile suspected in the recent terrorist bombings of two U.S. embassies in Africa, tried to obtain components of nuclear weapons and enriched uranium for the purpose of developing such weapons. U.S. District Court papers charge Mamdouh Mahmud Salim, allegedly a bin Laden lieutenant, with murder conspiracy and conspiracy to use weapons of mass destruction against U.S. nationals. The allegations against Salim, who may have helped to establish bin Laden's terrorist organization, Al Qaeda, are discussed.

Keyword(s): nuclear weapons of mass destruction; antiterrorism; combating terrorism; CBRNC

Mann, Paul. "Government/Industry Alliance Urged Against Cyber Threats," Aviation Week and Space Technology, 149, No. 2, July 13, 1998, 65-67.

President Clinton has introduced a landmark strategy to meet the threat of cyber and other unconventional terrorist attacks on the nation's computer systems and basic physical plants, including defense, aviation, and telecommunications. The strategy is intended to create a government/industry alliance to fend off computer hackers and other forms of terrorist attack on the nation's economic underpinnings. Security experts support the president's approach. They caution, however, that the success of the strategy, which is officially titled Presidential Decision Directive 63, will hinge on unparalleled public and private sector cooperation.

Keyword(s): cyberterrorism; antiterrorism; infrastructure protection; counterterrorism; combating terrorism

Mann, Paul. "Strategists Question U.S. Steadfastness," Aviation Week and Space Technology, 149, No. 9, August 31, 1998, 32-35.

To be effective, President Clinton's declared war on terrorism will require a sustained campaign using aerial bombing and ground forces, not only missile attacks like those against Sudan and Afghanistan, strategists say. Security experts are worried about U.S. follow-through over the long-term. They say neither the Pentagon nor the U.S. public has the stomach for using all of the antiterrorism tools at U.S. disposal, including commando raids by Special Operations Forces that would risk casualties and the taking of U.S. prisoners of war. Other experts were less certain, however, about the efficacy of a commando assault.

Keyword(s): combating terrorism; counterterrorism; antiterrorism

Mann, Paul. "Warnings Raised about Iraqi Terrorism Threat," Aviation Week and Space Technology, 148, No. 5, February 2, 1998, 22-23.

Iraq may threaten or even carry out a terrorist biological or chemical attack if Washington gives Baghdad an ultimatum to comply with United Nations weapons inspections, according to security specialists. They disagree on the probability of such a threat and Iraq's capability to fulfill it, but they declare that America should be getting ready for such a contingency and that its ability to respond is seriously lacking, both at home and overseas. David A. Kay, formerly chief weapons inspector for the UN Special Commission on Iraq, notes that missile warheads should not be viewed as the sole means of delivery for an Iraqi terrorist act.

Keyword(s): terrorism; CBRNC; chemical terrorism; nuclear terrorism; biological weapons of mass destruction; chemical weapons of mass destruction; biological terrorism; combating terrorism; antiterrorism; counterterrorism

Margeride, Jean-Baptiste. "Produits toxiques et biologiques: Armes de terrorisme," Strategique, [Paris], No. 2, 1995, 139-52 [in French].

This article reports on chemical and biological weapons used by or available to various countries or terrorist groups. There is some focus on the Aum Shinrikyo's sarin gas attack on the Tokyo subway system in 1995.

Keyword(s): technology; CBRNC; chemical weapons of mass destruction; biological terrorism; chemical terrorism; biological weapons of mass destruction

Martin, Daniel. "Cyber-terrorisme: Le nouveau peril," Politique Internationale, [Paris], Fall 1997 [in French], 299-312.

This article discusses the vulnerability of the information systems of major corporations, state administrations, and public authorities to attacks by individuals, terrorist groups, and outlaw states. The article is international in scope.

Keyword(s): technology; cyberterrorism; counterterrorism; combating terrorism

Matthew, Richard A. and George E. Shambaugh. "Sex, Drugs, and Heavy Metal: Transnational Threats and National Vulnerabilities," Security Dialogue, 29, No. 2, 1998, 163-77.

The article provides a background of globalized security threats of various types, including drug trafficking, infectious diseases, and terrorism thriving on arms proliferation. To improve security, the authors urge formation of counter threat centers to analyze transnational links upon which many such threats are based, combining the expertise of government agencies from all affected countries.

Keyword(s): future trends; antiterrorism; terrorism (general)

Medd, Roger, and Frank Goldstein. "International Terrorism on the Eve of a New Millennium," Studies in Conflict and Terrorism, [London], 20, No. 3, July-September 1997, 281-316.

The authors review the international terrorist activities of the last half century in order to make a case for needed changes in U.S. efforts to curb the growth of terrorism. They posit that a unified front against global terrorism is needed. Instead of focusing on how to respond during or after a terrorist incident, they examine measures for averting international terrorism disasters before they occur. The believe that, with the growing availability of weapons of mass destruction and computer technology to terrorist and organized crime groups, the risks are becoming too great to continue with a reactive approach to terrorism. The article begins with a discussion of how the basis for international terrorism has changed since its modern form began in the 1960s. It then extrapolates the evolutionary trend of terrorism to make projections for what can be expected in the future. Finally, it presents a number of practical ideas for preventing terrorist actions before they occur, beginning with an argument for redefining terrorism in terms that enable policy makers to organize more effectively against it. The article includes six figures and one table.

Keyword(s): terrorism; combating terrorism; counterterrorism

Messmer, Ellen. "Facts Fight Fiction in Security Circles," Network World, 15, No. 10, March 9, 1998, 1, 14.

The article discusses several favorite subjects in infowar circles. One concerns High-Energy Radio Frequency (HERF) guns, which are electromagnetic pulse weapons used to garble data stored on hard disks or tapes. HERF guns can also be used to temporarily disable networks by disrupting the electronic flow. Some suspect HERF guns were used against Saddam Hussein in the 1990-91 Gulf War and may be used in future conflicts. Another favorite subject is the U.S. National Security Administration (NSA). Within the European Parliament in Brussels, there has been growing concern about the U.S. power to intercept satellite communications via Echelon, the NSA's surveillance system that dates back to the 1980s. Another popular subject of speculation is whether Internet hackers are in league with Iraq's

Hussein.

Keyword(s): technology; cyberterrorism; information warfare; counterterrorism; antiterrorism; combating terrorism

Mickolus, Edward F., and Susan L. Simmons. Terrorism, 1992-1995: A Chronology of Events and a Selectively Annotated Bibliography. Westport, Connecticut and London: Greenwood Press, 1997. [Call Number: HV6431.M499 1997]

The book is a detailed account of terrorist events between 1992 and 1995. It provides specific names, places, strategies, weapons, and targets for attacks all over the world. Included are episodes of industrial and environmental terrorism as well as individual and group political actions, with a complete picture of motivations and circumstances for each as well as events resulting from terrorist acts and unfulfilled threats of such acts.

Keyword(s): terrorism (general); terrorist groups and activities

Milstein, Mark. H. "Nuclear and Present Danger: The Threat of Atomic Terrorism," Soldier of Fortune, 22, May 1997, 28-31.

The article discusses efforts to control the spread of nuclear materials and technology by national and international law enforcement and counterterrorism agencies, focusing on the U.S. Department of Energy's semisecret Nuclear Emergency Search Team (NEST). It also discusses reports on security at the atomic power plant in Paks, Hungary. It assesses the likelihood of an atomic weapon or radioactive-contamination device being assembled and used by a terrorist group.

Keyword(s): technology; combating terrorism; counterterrorism; nuclear terrorism; CBRNC

Morel, Benoit. "Chemical/Biological Terrorism: A New Problem That Calls for a New Medicine," Politics and the Life Sciences, [London], 15, September 1996, 207-8.

This article is a commentary on Jonathan B. Tucker's "Chemical/Biological Terrorism: Coping with a New Threat" (see Tucker, Jonathan B.). Benoit Morel argues that to fully combat chemical and biological terrorism, a new kind of international agreement is required, an agreement under which governments promise to help each other identify groups attempting to secretly produce chemical and biological compounds by opening their societies and allowing cooperation among law enforcers. Morel contends that chemical and biological weapons tend to be dealt with together but that, in the area of terrorism, they are very different and raise extremely diverse challenges.

Keyword(s): technology; CBRNC; chemical terrorism; biological terrorism; biological weapons of mass destruction; chemical weapons of mass destruction; counterterrorism; combating terrorism

Morris, Peter, and Steve Gold. "Cyber Terrorism," <u>Secure Computing</u>, July 1, 1997, 20-2, 25-7.

The article defines cyberterrorism broadly as the threat from information technology (IT)-based attacks on the integrity of an organization's IT system. Managers face cyberterrorism threats from many different directions, including remote (Internet-based) attacks, neo-Nazi groups operating on the Internet, subversion from current and former employees, as well as hackers. It says that hacking is not just about obtaining information, but is about instilling fear and doubt and compromising the integrity of the data. It reports that there have been attacks on financial institutions and the U.S. Department of Defense. It describes the use of the Internet and private bulletin board by terrorists to disseminate information. It discusses Freedom of Information and how public opinion since the bombings in Oklahoma City and at the World Trade Center has gone from an emphasis on complete freedom to support for responsible safeguards.

Keyword(s): technology; cyberterrorism; antiterrorism; combating terrorism

Morrocco, John D. "Hardening Concepts Tested to Counter Terrorist Blasts," <u>Aviation Week and Space Technology</u>, 146, No. 23, June 2, 1997, 44-45.

Preliminary results of an experiment by British and U.S. aviation security specialists validate new hardening concepts for civil aircraft to prevent catastrophic failure in the event of an internal explosion from a terrorist bomb. The test was the culmination of an $8.25-million, five-year research program by Britain's Civil Aviation Authority.

Keyword(s): technology; aviation security; terrorism; combating terrorism; antiterrorism

Morth, Todd A. "Considering Our Position: Viewing Information Warfare as a Use of Force Prohibited by Article 2(4) of the U.N. Charter," <u>Case Western Reserve Journal of International Law</u>, 30, Nos. 2/3, Spring/Summer 1998, 567-600.

Information networks have led to numerous advances in the quality of life by improving the provision of vital services such as electric power, medicine, and public safety. However, dependence on information networks also places those reliant on them in a position of vulnerability. If vital information networks stopped functioning, an information-age society would be paralyzed and could quickly collapse into chaos. Information warfare (IW) is troublesome for the international community because relative to chemical, biological, or nuclear weapons, the technology required to attack information networks is simple to acquire. The current state of international politics, with the demise of the Soviet Union as a superpower and the United Nations coalition victory in the 1991 Gulf War, has created a situation where nonconventional means, such as terrorism or IW, offer the best mechanism to attack the advanced Western countries. The United States and several European countries have recognized the potential threat posed by IW and are developing their own IW capabilities in answer to the threat. The article considers whether the international community should view IW as a prohibited use of force under Article 2(4) of the United Nations charter.

Keyword(s): information warfare; biological terrorism; CBRNC; chemical terrorism; chemical weapons of mass destruction; nuclear terrorism; nuclear weapons of mass destruction; antiterrorism; combating terrorism; biological weapons of mass destruction

Mullins, Wayman C. "An Organizational Perspective." Pages 127-68 in A Sourcebook on Domestic and International Terrorism: An Analysis of Issues, Organizations, Tactics, and Responses. 2d ed. Springfield, IL: Charles C. Thomas, 1997. [Call Number: HV6432.M86 1997]

This chapter highlights the organizational structure that terrorists use, among them the closed, circular structure in contrast with classic open bureaucratic structure. The nature of terrorist organizations makes it difficult to gain intelligence about terrorist activities, necessitating different and more comprehensive approaches to intelligence gathering. Topics discussed include The Circular Organization, Cellular Structure of the Terrorist Organization, Financing Terrorism, and Training of Terrorists. [lb]

Keyword(s): combating terrorism; counterterrorism; intelligence; terrorist groups and activities

Mullins, Wayman C. "Counter-terrorism and Legal Issues." Pages 358-95 in A Sourcebook on Domestic and International Terrorism: An Analysis of Issues, Organizations, Tactics, and Responses. 2d ed. Springfield, IL:
Charles C. Thomas, 1997. [Call Number: HV 6432.M86 1997]

This chapter explores the alternatives open to the United States in stopping terrorism, the response options open to the government and law enforcement agencies, and the legal measures that have been taken to control terrorist behavior. These responses range from passive to active. The discussion includes intelligence issues, political responses, covert operations, military responses, and U.S. domestic and international legal measures to counter terrorism. [lb]

Keyword(s): combating terrorism; counterterrorism; intelligence

Mullins, Wayman C. "Hostage Taking." Pages 437-75 in A Sourcebook on Domestic and International Terrorism: An Analysis of Issues, Organizations, Tactics, and Responses. 2d ed. Springfield, IL: Charles C. Thomas, 1997. [Call Number: HV6432.M86 1997]

This chapter discusses the only terrorist operation law enforcement has the opportunity to intercede in--the hostage situation. Hostage situations are resolved by long and complex negotiations. The author explains the negotiation process, the requirements for negotiating the hostage incident, handling demand issues, and how to make the negotiation process work against the terrorist. [lb]

Keyword(s): combating terrorism; terrorism; terrorist groups and activities

Mullins, Wayman C. "Nuclear, Biological, and Chemical Terrorism." Pages 323-57 in <u>A Sourcebook on Domestic and International Terrorism: An Analysis of Issues, Organizations, Tactics, and Responses</u>. 2d ed. Springfield, IL: Charles C. Thomas, 1997. [Call Number: HV 6432.M86 1997]

This chapter provides an overview of the newest and deadliest weapons in the terrorist's arsenal--weapons of mass destruction. The author finds that nuclear weapons have a low probability of usage. Biological weapons have a greater chance of employment, but chemical agents are the most likely weapons of mass destruction to be employed by terrorists at the present time. [lb]

Keyword(s): technology; nuclear terrorism; CBRNC; chemical/biological attacks

Mullins, Wayman C. "Terrorist Motivation and Psychology." Pages 86-126 in <u>A Sourcebook on Domestic and International Terrorism: An Analysis of Issues, Organizations, Tactics, and Responses</u>. 2d ed. Springfield, IL: Charles C. Thomas, 1997. [Call Number: HV 6432.M86 1997]

The author explores the reasons why people become terrorists, what motivates them to work outside acceptable guidelines of behavior, why they freely engage in violence, and the psychological characteristics of both terrorists and terrorist leaders. Although there are similarities between terrorists, there are significant differences. Varied goals dictate different targets, different strategies, and different tactics, all of which need to be taken into account when planning responses to terrorists.

Keyword(s): combating terrorism; terrorism; terrorist groups and activities

Mullins, Wayman C. "Terrorist Targets." Pages 237-86 in <u>A Sourcebook on Domestic and International Terrorism: An Analysis of Issues, Organizations, Tactics, and Responses</u>. 2d ed. Springfield, IL: Charles C. Thomas, 1997. [Call Number: HV6432.M86 1997]

The author discusses the strategy and tactics of terrorism, examining the types of operations terrorists employ and the intended outcomes of these operations. His basic point is that if terrorism is to be prevented, it is essential to understand how and why terrorists employ the types of operations they do and what purpose these operations are designed to accomplish. He also discusses hate crimes, terrorist involvement with drug traffic, and the role of the media in abetting and controlling terrorism. [lb]

Keyword(s): combating terrorism; counterterrorism; terrorist groups and activities

Mullins, Wayman C. "Terrorist Weapons." Pages 287-322 in <u>A Sourcebook on Domestic and International Terrorism: An Analysis of Issues, Organizations, Tactics, and Responses</u>. 2d ed. Springfield, IL: Charles C. Thomas, 1997. [Call Number: HV 6432.M86 1997]

The author provides an overview of the more conventional weapons that terrorists use, including a discussion of how they are obtained, made, and used. They are of two basic types--firearms and explosives, the terrorist's weapons of choice because they produce fear, are easy to obtain or make, require no special expertise, and are easy to conceal and transport. [lb]

Keyword(s): technology; combating terrorism; counterterrorism; terrorist groups and activities


Mullins, Wayman C. "The Future of Terrorism." Pages 476-522 in A Sourcebook on Domestic and International Terrorism: An Analysis of Issues, Organizations, Tactics, and Responses. 2d ed. Springfield, IL: Charles C. Thomas, 1997. [Call Number: HV 6432.M86 1997]

This chapter examines the future of terrorism in the United States as well as in the major geographic regions of the world. The author attempts to identify future terrorists, their targets, their base of operations, how they will attempt to achieve their objectives, and he predicts that incidents of terrorism will increase in the immediate years ahead. He also predicts that nuclear, biological, and chemical weapons will become standard weapons in the terrorist's arsenal and concludes that knowledge about terrorists and their methods and goals is essential if terrorism is to be defeated. [lb]

Keyword(s): future trends; terrorist groups and activities; combating terrorism


New Scientist. "Strike at Will," New Scientist, [London], 157, No. 2126, March 21, 1998, 3.

The writer discusses the difficulties associated with preparing for attacks on cities by terrorists equipped with biological weapons. In many large cities throughout the world, emergency services have made plans to deal with bioterrorist attacks. Despite these plans, there are real worries that no one can really predict just what type of incident could come next and how to cope with it effectively. The more we prepare for bioterrorist attacks, the worse it all seems. The fact remains that many deadly agents are available from hospitals or laboratories that could, in the hands of anyone with some kind of university-level knowledge of microbiology, be made in useful amounts. Unlike "conventional" extremists who are after political goals, the new breed of terrorists may simply be out to punish society or settle a grudge. The article concludes that there will be no quick fixes for the threats from bioterrorism.

Keyword(s): biological terrorism; CBRNC; biological weapons of mass destruction; counterterrorism; combating terrorism; antiterrorism; weapons of mass destruction in urban areas


Noah, D.L., A.L. Sobel, S.M. Ostroff, and J.A. Kildew. "Biological Warfare Training: Infectious Disease Outbreak Differentiation Criteria," Military Medicine, 163, No. 4, April 1998, 198-201.

The threat of biological terrorism and warfare may increase as the availability of weaponizable agents increases, the relative production costs of these agents decrease, and, most importantly, there exist terrorist groups willing to use them. Therefore, an important consideration is the ability to differentiate between natural and intentional outbreaks. Certain attributes of a disease outbreak may combine to provide convincing evidence of intentional causation. These potentially differentiating criteria include the proportion of combatants at risk, number of cases, geographic location, concurrence with belligerent activities of potential adversaries, and so forth.

Keyword(s): biological terrorism; CBRNC; antiterrorism; combating terrorism; biological agent detection; biological attacks; biological decontamination

Noble, Ronald K. "A Neglected Anti-Terror Weapon," New York Times, September 9, 1998, A25.

One step that the United States can take to increase its ability to catch international criminals and terrorists is to strengthen Interpol, the world's largest international police organization, embracing 177 countries. Fighting terrorism requires a lot of routine but important police work--tracking suspects, following leads, and uncovering criminal patterns. The best way to do this work is to rely on domestic law enforcement offices throughout the world. Interpol was created for this very purpose. Through its headquarters in Lyons, France, Interpol is linked to domestic police forces throughout the world. In theory, each local police agency should be able to communicate directly with the others in a matter of seconds. Sometimes the system works. Interpol also regularly issues notices on the possible whereabouts of dangerous fugitives.

Keyword(s): combating terrorism; counterterrorism; antiterrorism


Office of Intelligence and Threat Analysis, Bureau of Diplomatic Security. Significant Incidents of Political Violence Against Americans 1997. Washington, D.C.: U.S. Department of State, 1998.

This annual publication is intended to provide a comprehensive picture of the broad spectrum of political violence that American citizens and interests encountered abroad during 1997. In addition to examining terrorism-related acts, it also includes other instances of violence affecting Americans. The chronology is designed to encompass major anti-U.S. incidents that occurred in 1997. The selection of incidents used in the study is based on lethality, substantial property damage, use of unusual tactics or weapons, and perceptibility of targets as United States or representative of U.S. interests. In 1997, of the 135 incidents that involved U.S. citizens and interests, 127 specifically targeted Americans. The 135 incidents included 91 in Latin America, five in Sub-Saharan Africa, five in East Asia and the Pacific, 23 in Europe, seven in Near East Asia, and four in South Asia.

Keyword(s): antiterrorism; combating terrorism; counterterrorism


Osterman, Joseph. "Who Will Answer the Chem/Bio Call?," U.S. Naval Institute Proceedings, 122, December 1996, 37-40.

The author contends that the United States is unprepared to deal with terrorist attacks that use chemical and biological weapons. Thus, there is a need for the Department of Defense to begin planning, coordinating, and training to counter the threat. The article examines current United States domestic disaster planning and response, including roles of the Federal Bureau of Investigation (FBI), the Federal Emergency Management Agency (FEMA), the American Red Cross, and the armed forces, including the U.S. Marine Corps Biological/Chemical Incident Response Team.

Keyword(s): biological terrorism; biological weapons of mass destruction; chemical terrorism; chemical weapons of mass destruction

Paige, Sean. "Cover Story: Thinking the Unthinkable," Insight, 14, No. 3, January 26, 1998, 8.

Europe and many other parts of the world have long been plagued by acts of terrorism. But the growing threat of chemical and biological terrorism has U.S. officials fearing the worst.

Keyword(s): CBRNC; chemical weapons of mass destruction; biological terrorism; chemical terrorism; antiterrorism; combating terrorism; biological weapons of mass destruction

Patrick, William C., III. "Biological Terrorism and Aerosol Dissemination," Politics and the Life Sciences, [London], 15, September 1996, 208-10.

The writer discusses the problems encountered by terrorists in the dissemination of biological agents. Procedures and apparatuses for manufacturing liquid biological agents are simple, but the resulting product is quite difficult to disseminate into small particle, infectious aerosols. Conversely, procedures for producing dried biological agents are more intricate and require more advanced equipment. However, this product is easily disseminated by any number of crude devices.

Keyword(s): technology; biological terrorism; biological weapons of mass destruction; biological agent detection; biological attacks; CBRNC; counterterrorism; combating terrorism

Pearson, Graham S. "Chemical/Biological Terrorism: How Serious a Risk?," Politics and the Life Sciences, [London], 15, September 1996, 210-12.

This article is a commentary on Jonathan B. Tucker's "Chemical/Biological Terrorism: Coping with a New Threat" (see Tucker, Jonathan B.). Graham S. Pearson contends that although a number of important policy issues have been raised by Tucker about the potential threat of chemical and biological (C/B) terrorism, there are other important aspects that must be included in considerations of the seriousness of a risk posed by C/B terrorism. In addition, Pearson argues that there are other steps that can usefully be followed to lessen the risk of C/B terrorism. He asserts that it is advisable to devise and prepare a strategy to counter C/B terrorism because there can be no certainty that terrorists will follow a rational approach. He reexamines the short- and long-term policy steps proposed by Tucker for the United States for their totality and their wider applicability.

Keyword(s): CBRNC; chemical weapons of mass destruction; biological weapons of mass destruction; counterterrorism; combating terrorism

Pilat, Joseph F. "Chemical and Biological Terrorism after Tokyo: Reassessing Threats and Responses," Politics and the Life Sciences, [London], 15, September 1996, 213-15.

This article is a commentary on Jonathan B. Tucker's "Chemical/Biological Terrorism: Coping with a New Threat" (see Tucker, Jonathan B.). Although Tucker's conclusions appear to be accurate and his assessment of the prospects for future terrorism are strongly suggested throughout his article, he does not clearly and explicitly declare the reasoning behind these conclusions. The Tokyo subway gassing and its implications need to be properly understood in order to deal effectively with the nuclear, biological, and chemical (NBC) terrorism threat. Further analysis is needed of the central issues, ranging from the prevention of chemical and biological acquisition and use to protection during and following an attack. Nevertheless, Tucker's article soberly evaluates the threat of NBC terrorism and suggests a well-considered and realistic set of response options that will further the public debate on these issues.

Keyword(s): CBRNC; chemical weapons of mass destruction; biological weapons of mass destruction; counterterrorism; combating terrorism


Pollitt, M.M. "Cyberterrorism: Fact or Fancy?," Computer Fraud and Security, February 1998, 8-10.

The article discusses the definition of cyberterrorism and its potential, and suggests an approach to minimizing its dangers. The definition of cyberterrorism used in the article combines the U.S. Department of State's definition of terrorism as politically motivated acts of violence against noncombatants with a definition of cyberspace as the computers, networks, programs, and data that make up the information infrastructure. The author's conclusion is that by limiting the physical capabilities of the information infrastructure one can limit its potential for physical destruction.

Keyword(s): technology; cyberterrorism; antiterrorism; combating terrorism


Ranger, Robin, and David Wiencek. The Devil's Brews II: Weapons of Mass Destruction and International Security. London: Centre for Defence and International Security Studies, 1997.

The monograph discusses threats from nuclear, chemical, biological, and radiological munitions, particularly from guided-missile delivery systems, as well as defenses and countermeasures.

Keyword(s): CBRNC; biological terrorism; nuclear terrorism; chemical terrorism; chemical, biological, nuclear agents; chemical weapons of mass destruction; biological weapons of mass destruction; chemical/biological decontamination


Ranger, Robin, ed. The Devil's Brews I: Chemical and Biological Weapons and Their Delivery Systems. London: Centre for Defence and International Security Studies, 1996.

The book discusses how nuclear, chemical, biological, and radiological munitions threaten international security. It examines challenges in detecting, intercepting, and destroying ballistic missiles and other delivery systems. It recommends strengthened diplomatic and arms control efforts and increased investment in military deterrence capabilities. It provides some focus on the danger of attack from terrorists and outlaw regimes.

Keyword(s): CBRNC; biological weapons of mass destruction; chemical weapons of mass destruction; chemical terrorism; biological terrorism; nuclear terrorism; combating terrorism; counterterrorism

Richardson, Louise. "Global Rebels: Terrorist Organizations as Trans-national Actors," Harvard International Review, 20, No. 4, Fall 1998, 52-56.

The widespread usage of the term "terrorism," in many contexts, has rendered the word almost meaningless. Today, its only universally understood connotation is so pejorative that even terrorists do not admit to being terrorists anymore. A glance at current usage reveals child abuse, racism, and gang warfare all incorrectly described as terrorism. Thus, if terrorism is to be analyzed in any meaningful way, it must be readily distinguishable from other forms of violence, especially other forms of political violence. The article focuses on the international connections among terrorists.

Keyword(s): terrorism; antiterrorism; combating terrorism

Richter, Paul. "Bin Laden May Use Stone Age Tactics to Elude High-Tech Hunt," Los Angeles Times, September 7, 1998, A1, A3.

The United States has fired cruise missiles at sites linked to Bin Laden in retaliation for the bombings of U.S. embassies in Kenya and Tanzania. Intelligence officials have used advanced surveillance techniques to monitor his conversations and track the movements of his followers. Even before the August 7 embassy bombings, they reportedly drew up plans to send U.S. forces to Afghanistan to extricate Bin Laden, but the proposal eventually was rejected. Yet Bin Laden, the Islamic extremist accused of masterminding not only the embassy attacks but other acts of terrorism from a command post in the Afghan mountains, appears to have a potent defense against the world's most fully equipped modern power, U.S. officials acknowledge. U.S. authorities have claimed early success in their pursuit of Bin Laden, with the apprehension of several key suspects in the embassy bombings. But Bin Laden's apparent ability to adopt a primitive survival strategy raises questions about whether the United States--in this antiterror campaign and those that are likely to follow--truly has the punitive power it claimed in August 1998 when it launched the 79 cruise missiles of "Operation Infinite Reach."

Keyword(s): combating terrorism; counterterrorism; terrorist groups and activities

Roberts, Brad, and Michael Moodie. Combating NBC Terrorism: An Agenda for Enhancing International Cooperation. Alexandria, Virginia: Chemical and Biological Arms Control Institute, 1998.

This is a report on the possibility and restrictions of international cooperation dealing with possible terrorist use of nuclear, biological, and chemical (NBC) weapons. The report addresses existing international cooperation regarding the problem of NBC terrorism and the need for and availability of additional cooperation.

Keyword(s): combating terrorism; antiterrorism; CBRNC; chemical weapons of mass destruction; biological weapons of mass destruction; nuclear weapons of mass destruction; counterterrorism

Roberts, Brad, ed. Terrorism with Chemical and Biological Weapons: Calibrating Risks and Responses. Alexandria, Virginia: Chemical and Biological Arms Control Institute, 1997.

This volume examines whether the taboo against terrorists using chemical and biological weapons has been broken. It analyzes the common features of terrorist groups that possibly would be willing to use chemical and biological weapons and the technical opportunities for and barriers against their use by terrorists. It also provides a description of critical policy tools for preventing terrorist uses of these weapons, as well as for meeting the challenge of chemical and biological terrorism.

Keyword(s): CBRNC; chemical weapons of mass destruction; biological terrorism; chemical terrorism; combating terrorism; counterterrorism; antiterrorism; biological weapons of mass destruction

Roberts, Brad. "Terrorism and Weapons of Mass Destruction: Has the Taboo Been Broken?," Politics and the Life Sciences, [London], 15, September 1996, 216-17.

This article is a commentary on Jonathan B. Tucker's "Chemical/Biological Terrorism: Coping with a New Threat" (see Tucker, Jonathan B.). Brad Roberts assesses Tucker's description of "a new type of terrorist." In deliberating about the future of chemical and biological weapons (CBW) terrorism, Roberts separates the problem into two parts: the part posed by traditional terrorist actors, either individuals or groups, who may see CBW as a new implement of warfare, and the part posed by new terrorist actors, who may consider CBW an appropriate instrument for new purposes. Roberts concludes that for traditional terrorist actors, considerable obstacles to the use of weapons of mass destruction endure because such weapons are essentially counterproductive for their proposed aims. However, for the nontraditional terrorist actors the taboo on the use of such weapons may not be in the least bit pertinent.

Keyword(s): CBRNC; chemical weapons of mass destruction; biological weapons of mass destruction; combating terrorism; counterterrorism

Rosenau, William G. ""Every Room Is a New Battle": The Lessons of Modern Urban Warfare," Studies in Conflict and Terrorism, [London], 20, No. 4, October-December 1997, 371-94.

The world is urbanizing rapidly, yet Western military forces have yet to come to terms with the peculiar demands of urban warfare. The harsh urban environment, particularly in the developing world, is an ideal arena for "asymmetrical" adversaries seeking to neutralize the technological, logistical, and organizational advantages currently enjoyed by modern military forces. After examining some of the security implications of urbanization, the author discusses three recent representative examples of urban warfare: Beirut, 1982; Mogadishu, 1993; and Grozny, 1994-95. In each case study, he examines the organization, equipment, and training of the forces involved, and draws conclusions about what types of military systems, munitions, and force structure were effective, and why. The remainder of the article draws together lessons from these case studies and from other accounts of urban battles in an effort to understand what is needed to improve military performance in this environment. He concludes that greater effectiveness will require changes in organization and equipment; more important, it will also require a change in a military organizational culture that has largely ignored the challenge of fighting an asymmetrical adversary on urban terrain.

Keyword(s): terrorism; combating terrorism; counterterrorism

Rowe, Richard. "Safety in Numbers," Airports International, May 1996, 13-16.

The article describes the current range of baggage security systems in use in international airports. It then proposes ways for individual systems to be streamlined and integrated with systems in existence at other international airports to achieve greater overall security. Also offered is a detailed evaluation of several security approaches as to their efficiency and their rate of rejection, together with a description of the attitudes of airlines toward today's security measures.

Keyword(s): inspection of aircraft cargo containers; inspection of aircraft carry-on luggage; future trends

Sandler, Todd. "On the Relationship between Democracy and Terrorism," Terrorism and Political Violence [London], 7, No. 4, Winter 1995, 1-9.

The article is a detailed analysis of the methodology and criteria used to classify groups as terrorist and countries as sources of terrorist activity. The basis for the discussion is the work of William Eubank and Leonard Weinberg on this subject. The article cites examples of countries where the terrorist classification encounters difficulties because of the nature of activity or other complications.

Keyword(s): terrorist groups and activities; terrorism (general)

Sanz, Timothy L.. "Nuclear Terrorism Bibliography: Nuclear Terrorism: Published Literature Since 1992," Military Review, 77, No. 4, July-August 1997, 139-48.

In compiling this extensive bibliography of articles and books on nuclear terrorism, the author used the research sources of a multitude of data bases, CD-ROMs, and indexes. A large part of this literature on this topic addresses the security of nuclear weapons in the former Soviet Union. Six other sections of the bibliography include works on threat assessments, threats by nation states, security of nuclear facilities, countermeasures/prevention, legal aspects of the problem, and World Wide Web sites. The bibliography includes a synopsis of publications of special relevance to defense officials.

Keyword(s): antiterrorism; counterterrorism; combating terrorism; technology; nuclear terrorism; nuclear weapons of mass destruction; CBRNC

Schwartz, Daniel M. "Environmental Terrorism: Analyzing the Concept," Journal of Peace Research, [London], 35, No. 4, 1998, 483-96.

Although the term "environmental terrorism" has found its way into North American politics, media, and academia, the concept remains ambiguous. The author asks when is it appropriate to call environmental destruction "environmental terrorism." He argues that the term has been widely misused. He devises a taxonomy that allows one to systematically discern the types of environmental destruction that can legitimately be labeled "terrorism" and those that can be labeled "environmental terrorism."

Keyword(s): CBRNC; biological terrorism; future trends; combating terrorism; antiterrorism; biological weapons of mass destruction

Schweitzer, Glenn E., with Carole C. Dorsh. Superterrorism: Assassins, Mobsters, and Weapons of Mass Destruction. New York: Plenum Publishing Corporation, 1998. [Call Number: HV6431 .S375 1998]

The book alerts the reader to the barrage of new terrorist threats targeted at Americans in the form of biological, chemical, and nuclear weapons. The author focuses on the volatile mix created when religious zealots join forces with mobsters, drawing on billions of dollars of laundered drug money to bankroll terrorist attacks. He warns that the tried-and-true routes for smuggling drugs and arms may become highways for contraband nuclear, chemical, and biological materials that could lead to the kind of holocaust that Americans have never known. Also, he exposes the unholy emerging alliances between American dissidents and international terrorist groups. With the latest technology in the hands of terrorists, the author signals the arrival of cyberterrorism. The author, director for Central Europe and Eurasia of the National Academy of Sciences, reveals that stocks of uranium and plutonium have disappeared from the former Soviet Union for unknown destinations. He bolsters his own revelations with scores of interviews with diplomats, intelligence operatives, and experts worldwide.

Keyword(s): CBRNC; combating terrorism; antiterrorism; counterterrorism; cyberterrorism; chemical weapons of mass destruction; nuclear weapons of mass destruction; biological weapons of mass destruction

Sharif, Idris. The Success of Political Terrorist Events: An Analysis of Terrorist Tactics and Victim Characteristics, 1968 to 1977. Lanham, Maryland: University Press of America, 1996. [Call Number: HV6431.S4665 1996]

The book provides a strong background on the psychological and political motivations of terrorist behavior, followed by a statistical analysis of terrorist actions in the period listed. Elements of that analysis are degrees of success, tactics, type of target, type of victim, geographical location, and weapons used. The likelihood of success for a future terrorist action is calculated using these variables.

Keyword(s): terrorism (general); terrorist groups and activities

Shelton, Lieutenant Colonel Raymond S. "No Democracy Can Feel Secure," U.S. Naval Institute Proceedings, 124, No. 1,146, 1998, 39-44.

Using as its premise that the U.S. Armed Forces will almost assuredly encounter a biological agent in the very near future, the article focuses on the challenge to train and equip U.S. troops to respond with efficiency and tenacity. Counterproliferation measures are extremely difficult because biological warfare (BW) programs are easily hidden within legitimate facilities. The article discusses active, passive, and medical defense measures, all of which depend heavily on intelligence. It concludes that the military can avoid the BW trap only through a concerted national effort at all levels, including the Joint Service Integration Group and the Joint Service Material Group.

Keyword(s): biological warfare; biological weapons of mass destruction; biological attacks; biological terrorism; biological agent detection; biological decontamination

Shenon, Philip. ""Report on Security Suggests Closing Some U. S. Embassies"," New York Times, January 9, 1999, A7.

This article presents the results of special panels set up by the State Department to investigate the bombings of embassies in Nairobi and Dar es Salaam in August 1998. The report accused the department of failure to recognize the seriousness of threats to its embassies and staff of transnational terrorists and truck bombs. It also cited the failure to train staff to deal with attacks and to take adequate steps to increase the physical security of embassy buildings. The report recommended creation of "super-embassies" in secure capitals that would manage diplomatic affairs for several countries as one way to protect against future terrorist attacks.

Keyword(s): antiterrorism; combating terrorism; future trends

Sherrow, Richard L. "Better Killing Chemistry: SOF Examines Weapons of Mass Destruction for Tiny Tyrants and Terrorists," Soldier of Fortune, 23, No. 9, September 1998, 32-35, 71.

The article discusses the history of chemical-biological warfare (CBW), CBW agents, choking agents, blood agents, blister agents, and nerve agents. It also summarizes CBW from World War I to the Vietnam War.

Keyword(s): CBRNC; biological weapons of mass destruction; terrorism; chemical terrorism; biological terrorism; chemical/biological attacks; chemical, biological, nuclear agents; chemical weapons of mass destruction

Shoham, Dany. "Chemical/Biological Terrorism: An Old, but Growing Threat in the Middle East and Elsewhere," Politics and the Life Sciences, [London], 15, September 1996, 218-19.

This article is a commentary on Jonathan B. Tucker's "Chemical/Biological Weapons: Coping with a New Threat" (see Tucker, Jonathan B.). Dany Shoham argues that chemical/biological (C/B) terrorism is not really a new threat but a growing threat that currently poses a danger that ought to be practically and expediently dealt with. He contends that the manufacture of C/B weapons by terrorists themselves is not as important as it appears to be in Tucker's analysis. In addition, Shoham considers the feasibility of domestic as opposed to foreign C/B terrorism. Furthermore, he criticizes Tucker's lack of an appropriate demonstration of a biological incident and challenges Tucker's technical information, omitted references, and the validity and completeness of data presented in his section on Israel. Shoham concludes that supreme attention must be paid to the likelihood that terrorists will try to follow the relative operational success that marked the initiatives recently taken in Japan.

Keyword(s): CBRNC; chemical weapons of mass destruction; biological weapons of mass destruction; counterterrorism; combating terrorism


Siegrist, David W.. Advanced Technology to Counter Biological Terrorism. Potomac Institute for Policy Studies, March 18, 1998.

This monograph assesses domestic and international terrorist threats and defenses, focusing chiefly on the United States and other Western countries. It discusses technical issues and nonmedical and advanced medical countermeasures.

Keyword(s): biological terrorism; CBRNC; combating terrorism; antiterrorism; biological agent detection; counterterrorism; biological weapons of mass destruction


Smithson, Amy E., and Laurie H. Boulden. "Chemical Weapons: Neglected Menace; U.S. Policymakers Are Not Taking the Threat of a Chemical Weapons Attack Seriously," Issues in Science and Technology, [London], 12, Spring 1996, 75-81.

The article discusses implications for international security of the weapons capability demonstrated by the 1996 Tokyo sarin gas attack. It advocates Clinton Administration pressure for ratification of the Chemical Weapons Convention (CWC).

Keyword(s): chemical terrorism; chemical attacks; chemical weapons of mass destruction; CBRNC; combating terrorism; counterterrorism


Smithson, Amy E. "The Politics of Chemical/Biological Counterterrorism: Addressing or Perpetuating U.S. Vulnerability?," Politics and the Life Sciences, [London], 15, September 1996, 220-1.

This article is a commentary on Jonathan B. Tucker's "Chemical/Biological Terrorism: Coping with a New Threat" (see Tucker, Jonathan B.). Tucker's suggestions for limiting and coping with the problem of chemical and biological weapons are realistic in that they are technically possible, politically attainable, and economically affordable. The U.S. Senate has been inactive on the Chemical Weapons Convention, but ideas resembling Tucker's recommendations are now beginning to appear. Details of such ideas, Tucker's proposals concerning the provision of incentives for the development of better antiviral and antibiotic drugs, and a counter argument to his view that the federal government's counterterrorism preparations should be kept "low-profile" so as not to rile those considering chemical or biological terrorism or arouse public fear are provided.

Keyword(s): CBRNC; chemical weapons of mass destruction; biological weapons of mass destruction; counterterrorism; combating terrorism; biological agent detection

Smyth, Frank. "Culture Clash: Bin Laden, Khartoum and the War Against the West," Jane's Intelligence Review, [London], 10, No. 10, October 1998, 22-25.

The author, who traveled north from Uganda into southern Sudan, examines Sudan's role as a rogue state in supporting radical Islamist groups such as Osama bin Laden's network. The author summarizes bin Laden's background and how he came to spend the period from 1991 to May 1996 in Sudan. The author notes that he does not know what, if any, ties the Sudanese regime may still have with bin Laden.

Keyword(s): counterterrorism; combating terrorism; terrorist groups and activities

Sopko, John F. "The Changing Proliferation Threat," Foreign Policy, Winter 1996/97, 3-20.

The article examines new terrorist threats to the United States in light of increased availability of nuclear, chemical, and biological weapons and the breakup of nations.

Keyword(s): CBRNC; biological terrorism; chemical terrorism

Staten, Clark L. "Asymmetric Warfare, the Evolution and Devolution of Terrorism: The Coming Challenge for Emergency and National Security Forces," http://www.emergency.com (Website), April 27, 1998, 1-7.

The author, executive director and senior analyst of the Emergency Response and Research Institute in Chicago, argues that the nature of global warfare is changing, and that there is a general paradigm shift underway in regard to how future conflicts will unfold. For the coming decade, he predicts an increasing number of "brush-fire" wars, counterinsurgency campaigns, hostage-rescue operations, "drug wars," low-intensity conflicts, urban combat, and "peacekeeping operations" that will require a vastly different set of tactics, equipment, training, and skills than conventional military engagements of the past. Future conflicts will likely involve combating small units of fanatical terrorists using weapons of mass destruction and other sophisticated tactics and technologies.

Keyword(s): future trends; CBRNC; technology; combating terrorism; counterterrorism; antiterrorism

Stern, Jessica Eve. "Op-Ed: Taking the Terror Out of Bioterrorism," <u>New York Times</u>, April 8, 1998, A19.

Although biological weapons can kill millions and are invisible and silent in the process, they don't warrant panic. They are relatively easy to grow or obtain, but they must be spread effectively. It would help if some measures were taken. Pharmaceuticals to counter the effects of biological agents can be stockpiled, and new drugs can be developed. The system for domestic and worldwide monitoring of disease outbreaks in humans, animals, and plants must be strengthened, and detectors capable of fast identification of biological agents must be developed and deployed. Most important may be finding employment for one-time Soviet biological weapons scientists, many of whom are now unemployed or underpaid.

Keyword(s): biological terrorism; CBRNC; combating terrorism; biological agent detection; antiterrorism; biological weapons of mass destruction

Stern, Jessica Eve. "Weapons of Mass Impact: A Growing and Worrisome Danger," <u>Politics and the Life Sciences</u>, [London], 15, September 1996, 222-25.

This article is a commentary on Jonathan B. Tucker's "Chemical/Biological Terrorism: Coping with a New Threat" (see Tucker, Jonathan B.). Jessica Stern notes that her commentary is less a critique than a supplementary debate as to whether terrorists are likely to use chemical weapons again after the sarin attack on the Tokyo subway in 1995, the kinds of strategy that they might adopt, and the types of terrorists most liable to resort to them. She agrees with Tucker that pressures against chemical and biological (C/B) terrorism continue to erode and that the possibility for C/B terrorism is increasing. In contrast with Tucker, she contends that because these weapons are intrinsically terrorizing, they are even better suited for attracting attention than for producing mass casualties.

Keyword(s): CBRNC; biological weapons of mass destruction; chemical weapons of mass destruction; combating terrorism; counterterrorism

Stock, Thomas. "Fighting CBW Terrorism: Means and Possibilities," <u>Politics and the Life Sciences</u>, [London], 15, September 1996, 225-7.

This article is a commentary on Jonathan B. Tucker's "Chemical/Biological Terrorism: Coping with a New Threat" (see Tucker, Jonathan B.). Tucker argues that there is a need to assess existing counterterrorism measures, in particular those for chemical and biological terrorism. The Chemical Weapons Convention (CWC), which is likely to be implemented soon, has the potential to diminish the risk of terrorist use of toxic chemicals, but the small quantities that might be useful to terrorists can never be totally restricted, particularly at the international level. Although the CWC will obstruct some of the potential routes that terrorists and rogue nations might follow to obtain chemical weapons, it is only in association with improved national law enforcement efforts and intelligence collection that the CWC can assist in fighting chemical terrorism.

Keyword(s): CBRNC; chemical weapons of mass destruction; biological weapons of mass destruction;

combating terrorism; counterterrorism


Stone, R. "An Antidote to Bioproliferation," Science, [London], 278, No. 5341, November 14, 1997, 1222.

A U.S. National Academy of Sciences (NAS) committee has urged the U.S. Department of Defense to launch a five-year, $38.5 million initiative to fund collaborations between Russian biological weapons experts and their U.S. counterparts. The committee is hoping to deter the Russian specialists from being lured to countries that sponsor terrorism.

Keyword(s): biological weapons of mass destruction; CBRNC; antiterrorism; combating terrorism; biological terrorism


Thranert, Oliver. "Biological Weapons and the Problems of Nonproliferation," Aussenpolitik, 48, No. 2, November 1997, 148-57.

By and large unnoticed by the general public, the instruments of biological warfare have developed into a new threat to international security. The author, a foreign and security policy expert at the Research Institute of the Friedrich Ebert Foundation in Bonn, takes a closer look at the problems involved and the means by which the international community is trying to respond to the new challenge. He concludes that the risk emanating from biological weapons is real and will probably tend to increase in the future. He advises taking resolute measures to strengthen the weak prohibitory regime for biological weapons and to continue to foster biological protection projects. He believes that recourse to nuclear arsenals to deter the use of biological weapons is highly problematic, because it could jeopardize the entire architecture of efforts aimed at the nonproliferation of weapons of mass destruction.

Keyword(s): CBRNC; biological weapons of mass destruction; antiterrorism; combating terrorism; biological terrorism


Thranert, Oliver. "Preemption, Civil Defense, and Psychological Analysis: Three Necessary Tools in Responding to Irrational Terrorism," Politics and the Life Sciences, [London], 15, September 1996, 228-30.

This article is a commentary on Jonathan B. Tucker's "Chemical/Biological Terrorism: Coping with a New Threat" (see Tucker, Jonathan B.). Tucker provides an excellent and precise analysis but, in comparison with his threat analysis, his policy suggestions are weak. Chemical and biological terrorism is new not so much because access to chemicals and biologicals is relatively easy but because there are new terrorist groups who simply want to kill people without having any rational restriction. To handle the hazard, a preemptive measure should be attempted, namely, providing for a civil defense as far as is possible. However, the resolution of the problem demands public debate to examine why such groups as Aum Shinrikyo in Japan can attract young educated people in modern industrial societies in the first place.

Keyword(s): CBRNC; biological weapons of mass destruction; chemical weapons of mass destruction;

counterterrorism; combating terrorism; antiterrorism

Tucker, Jonathan B. "Chemical/Biological Terrorism: Coping with a New Threat," Politics and the Life Sciences, [London],15, September 1996, 167-83.

In March 1995, Aum Shinrikyo terrorists released sarin in the Tokyo subway, causing 11 deaths and more than 5,000 injuries. Although terrorists have sought to acquire chemical/biological (C/B) agents in the past, and a few have employed them on a small scale, the Tokyo attack was the first large-scale terrorist use of a lethal chemical agent against unarmed civilians, weakening a longstanding psychological taboo. This tragic incident has therefore drawn worldwide attention to the emerging threat of C/B terrorism. Despite significant technical hurdles associated with the production and delivery of C/B agents, such weapons are within the reach of terrorist groups that possess the necessary scientific know-how and financial resources. This article proposes a C/B counterterrorism strategy based on preemption and civil defense, and recommends several short-term and longer-term policy options for mitigating this emerging threat.

Keyword(s): biological terrorism; chemical terrorism; biological weapons of mass destruction; chemical weapons of mass destruction; biological agent detection

Tucker, Jonathan B. "Measures to Fight Chemical/Biological Terrorism: How Little Is Enough?," Politics and the Life Sciences, [London], 15, September 1996, 240-47.

Tucker replies to 24 commentaries on his article "Chemical/Biological Terrorism: Coping with a New Threat" (see Tucker, Jonathan B.). He contends that the issue of possible motivations of terrorist organizations in resorting to chemical and biological (C/B) weapons is complex and that his analysis was simplistic in seeking to draw a sharp distinction between groups motivated by political ends versus religious or racist ideology. He argues that what is new about the threat of C/B terrorism is that it potentially grants a small number of individuals the capacity to disturb society on an immense scale. In addition, he asserts that the largest threat comes from terrorists motivated by religious fanaticism or racial hatred, who regard violence and murder directed against a specific race or class of people as justifiable. Finally, Tucker addresses some of the criticisms of his technical arguments and policy recommendations.

Keyword(s): chemical terrorism; biological terrorism; biological weapons of mass destruction; chemical weapons of mass destruction; counterterrorism; combating terrorism

Tucker, Jonathan B. "Putting Teeth in the Biological Weapons Ban," Technical Review, 100, January-February 1998, 38-45.

The article describes the deadly potential of disease-causing microbes such as anthrax in inflicting mass casualties and the consequent need for more effective control over biologically potent materials. The author notes the caveat that a balance must be found between the need for intrusive inspection procedures and the need to protect the trade secrets of biotechnical industries.

Keyword(s): biological terrorism; future trends; antiterrorism

Turpen, Elizabeth, and Steven P. Kadner. "Counterproliferation versus Nonproliferation: A Case for Prevention versus Post Factum Intervention," Fletcher Forum of World Affairs, 21, Winter/Spring 1997, 153-71.

The article discusses approaches to controlling development and use of nuclear, chemical, and biological weapons. It stresses the need for the United States to assume a strong leadership position.

Keyword(s): CBRNC; chemical weapons of mass destruction; biological weapons of mass destruction; chemical attacks; biological attacks; counterterrorism; combating terrorism

United States Department of State. Patterns of Global Terrorism 1997. Washington, D.C.: Department of State, 1996. [Call Number: HV6431.P377 1995]

This annual report describes events of terrorism for the year and also provides updates of the year's activities and status reports of known terrorist organizations and counterterrorist efforts, listed by country. A chronological listing of worldwide terrorist incidents also is provided, as is a brief statistical breakdown of incidents by region, type of target, and number of casualties. _ _

Keyword(s): terrorism (general); terrorist groups and activities

United States. Congress. 104th, 1st Session. Senate. Committee on the Judiciary. Subcommittee on Terrorism, Technology, and Government Information. The Availability of Bomb-Making Information on the Internet. Washington, D.C.: GPO, Superintendent of Documents, 1996.

The hearing examines types of "mayhem manuals" posted on the Internet, including instructions for explosive devices, in light of terrorist bombings and other incidents in the United States. Other issues discussed include the First Amendment, public protection, restricting children's access, censorship, and government regulation. The hearing also covers materials posted by militia, hate, and political extremist groups, and the alternative press.

Keyword(s): technology; cyberterrorism; CBRNC; nuclear terrorism

United States. Congress. 104th, 1st Session. Senate. Committee on the Judiciary. The Role of the Military in Combating Terrorism: Hearing, May 10, 1995, on Certain Provisions of S. 735, A Bill to Prevent and Punish Acts of Terrorism and Certain Provisions of S. 761, A Bill to Improve the Ability of the United States to Respond to the International Terrorist Threat. Washington, D.C.: GPO, Superintendent of Documents, 1996.

The hearing examines the proper role, if any, of the U.S. military in countering terrorism. It provides special focus on the Posse Comitatus Act.

Keyword(s): counterterrorism; combating terrorism; terrorism


United States. Congress. 106th, 1st Session. Senate. Senate Judiciary Subcommittee on Technology, Terrorism, and Government; Senate Select Committee on Intelligence. Biological Weapons: The Threat Posed by Terrorist.*. Washington, D.C.: GPO, Superintendent of Documents, March 4, 1998..

These are transcripts of Colonel David Franz's and two others' testimonies before Senate committees. Franz defines biological terrorism and differentiates biological agents from chemical ones. He offers threat assessments and concludes that preparing medical and health sectors as well as educating the public will go far to reduce the effectiveness of a biological attack. Dr. Stephen M. Ostroff of the Center for Disease Control (CDC) describes the CDC's role as regulating the shipment of certain biological agents that are capable of causing substantial harm to human health. Ostroff also addresses the adequacy and effectiveness of other safeguards to prevent the use of dangerous biological agents. W. Seth Carus offers his assessment of the biological terrorist threat. Perhaps his most poignant statement is that "pound for pound, [biological agents] are potentially more lethal than thermonuclear weapons."

Keyword(s): CBRNC; biological weapons of mass destruction; biological terrorism; antiterrorism; combating terrorism

United States. Department of State. Office of Intelligence and Threat Analysis. Significant Incidents of Political Violence against Americans: 1996. Washington, D.C.: Department of State, 1997.

The book is an annual account of incidents involving Americans in all parts of the world. Included are a wide variety of violent incidents, many of which fit the definition of terrorism (planting of bombs, kidnaping). A statistical analysis is given by region and by type of attack; incidents are summarized briefly.

Keyword(s): terrorism (general); terrorist groups and activities


Vachon, Gordon K. "Responding to the Threat of Chemical/Biological Terrorism: International Dimensions Revisited," Politics and the Life Sciences, [London], 15, September 1996, 230-32.

This article is a commentary on Jonathan B. Tucker's "Chemical/Biological Terrorism: Coping with a New Threat" (see Tucker, Jonathan B.). Tucker's article lays a solid basis for an enlightened and undoubtedly lively debate on policy prescriptions to address chemical and biological terrorist threats. It suggests that the March 1995 sarin incident in Tokyo has had a certain impact on the chemical and biological terrorism landscape, definitely for ill and possibly, if the relevant lessons are learned, for some good in terms of future preparedness.

Keyword(s): CBRNC; chemical weapons of mass destruction; biological weapons of mass destruction; chemical terrorism; biological terrorism; combating terrorism; counterterrorism

Van Atta, Dale. "Carbombs and Cameras: The Need for Responsible Media Coverage of Terrorism," Harvard International Review, 20, No. 4, Fall 1998, 66-70.

It is in the nature of most terrorists, like serial murderers, to crave publicity. Neither can achieve their objective without it. The primary purpose is to create a sensational event that affects entire populations, and this is best achieved through the media. The article presents a discussion of terrorism and publicity, with an emphasis on the case of Osama bin Laden.

Keyword(s): terrorism; terrorist cults; antiterrorism; combating terrorism

Venter, Al J. "Poisoned Chalice Poses Problems: The Terrorist Threat to the World's Water," Jane's International Defense Review, [London], 32, No. 1, January 1999, 57-61.

Recent U.S. intelligence reports indicate that water supplies in Africa and even Bosnia could become terrorist targets in the future. There are about 20 documented instances of the use (or the threat) of chemical or biological agents against water supplies. A thesis completed at the Naval Postgraduate School, Monterey, California, by U.S. Navy Lieutenant Commander William Monday, entitled "Thinking the Unthinkable: Attacking Fresh Water Supplies," contends that not only is an attack on water possible, but it also has the potential to achieve mass casualties if properly planned and executed. A number of biological and chemical agents are capable of surviving in treated (chlorinated) water, including anthrax. Detection remains inadequate. The article includes background on biological and chemical threats to water supply.

Keyword(s): technology; CBRNC; biological weapons of mass destruction; chemical weapons of mass destruction; antiterrorism; combating terrorism; biological agent detection; future trends; terrorism; biological terrorism

Wall, Robert. "Advance Technology To Protect High- and Low-Risk Facilities," Aviation Week and Space Technology, 149, No. 7, August 17, 1998, 72-73.

Joint Chiefs of Staff Chairman General Henry Shelton, the nation's top soldier, says that improving the defenses of high-risk overseas U.S. facilities has driven terrorists to attack more poorly defended, low-threat sites. U.S. researchers are trying to quickly develop advanced equipment to lessen vulnerabilities at high- and low-risk facilities. The U.S. Air Force is conducting demonstrations of new technology, such as unmanned aerial vehicles and explosives detectors, as part of an overall Pentagon effort to strengthen the defenses of forward-operating bases.

Keyword(s): combating terrorism; counterterrorism; antiterrorism

Waller, Douglas. "Inside the Hunt for Osama," Time, December 21, 1998, 32-36.

U.S. federal agents have trailed Osama bin Laden and his secret network for years. Many observers wonder why they did not stop the bombings of the U.S. embassies in Kenya and Tanzania in August

1998. The article looks at some of bin Laden's activities over the past years.

Keyword(s): antiterrorism; combating terrorism; terrorism; terrorist groups and activities; counterterrorism

Wark, William B. "Managing the Consequences of Nuclear, Biological, and Chemical (NBC) Terrorism," Low Intensity Conflict and Law Enforcement, [London], 6, No. 2, Autumn 1997, 179-84.

This article outlines U.S. roles and responsibilities in dealing with the consequences of terrorism. Managing the consequences of nuclear, biological, and chemical (NBC) terrorism falls within the jurisdiction of the Federal Emergency Management Agency (FEMA). The author concludes that FEMA is not as ready to manage the consequences of NBC terrorism as it would like to be, and that FEMA needs improved planning, communication, cooperation, and coordination both internationally and on the federal, state, and local levels. He also sees a need to heighten public awareness of the terrorist threat.

Keyword(s): CBRNC; biological weapons of mass destruction; chemical weapons of mass destruction; biological terrorism; chemical terrorism; combating terrorism; counterterrorism

Weinberg, Leonard B., and William L. Eubank. "Terrorism and Democracy: What Recent Events Disclose," Terrorism and Political Violence, [London], 10, No. 1, Spring 1998, 108-118.

The authors explore relationships between terrorism and democracy by making use of the Rand-St. Andrews Chronology of International Terrorism for 1994. The authors use these data sets to determine if there is a linkage between the occurrence of terrorist attacks and the type of incumbent political regime in the countries where this terrorism is perpetrated. For the two classifications of political regimes, they draw from Robert Wesson's 1987 study Democracy: A Worldwide Survey and the Freedom House publication Freedom in the World for 1984-85 and 1994-95, in order to evaluate the impact of regime change on the incidence of terrorist events. Their principal finding, consistent with earlier work, is that terrorist events are substantially more likely to occur in free and democratic settings than in any of the alternatives. They discover, however, that change in and of itself makes a difference. Countries that underwent change in the period under consideration were more likely to experience terrorism than countries that did not.

Keyword(s): antiterrorism; combating terrorism; terrorism

Whitelaw, Kevin. "Terrorists on the Web: Electronic 'Safe Haven'," U.S. News and World Report, 124, No. 24, June 22, 1998, 46.

At least 12 of the 30 organizations on the U.S. Department of State's list of terrorist organizations have their own Web sites. Officials think some terrorists may use encoded e-mail to plan attacks, but the groups mostly use the sites for transmitting propaganda. Forcing terrorist groups to shut down these sites is not an option, because it would be extremely difficult to carry out, legally questionable, and a violation of the Internet's freewheeling culture.

Keyword(s): cyberterrorism; terrorist groups and activities; combating terrorism; antiterrorism

Wilcox, Jr., Philip C. "The Western Alliance and the Challenge of Combating Terrorism," Terrorism and Political Violence, [London], 9, No. 4, Winter 1997, 1-7.

The author begins by seeking to explain why terrorism has risen higher in the hierarchy of "global issues" at a time when the trend in international terrorist incidents (those involving the territory or citizens of more than one country) is declining. The second part of the article surveys what the Western Alliance is doing to combat terrorism, and concludes that although much has been achieved by improved international cooperation in counterterrorism more efforts are needed to deal with crises and conflicts that, if left to languish, can lead to violence and terrorism.

Keyword(s): terrorism; combating terrorism; counterterrorism

Wilkinson, Paul. "How to Combat the Reign of Terror: The Recent Spate of Terrorist Attacks Prompts the Question: How Can the International Community Ensure Global Security?," New Statesman, [London], 125, August 2, 1996, 12-13.

The author discusses how the international community can ensure global security in the light of a recent spate of terrorist attacks. There is room for improved cooperation in relation to such areas as intelligence sharing and disrupting the financial structures and fund-raising activities of terrorist groups. A concerted, multipronged approach is required that is carefully calibrated to the level required to deal with the scale of terrorism used and that combines the most vital elements of political, legal, police, and socioeconomic measures. Bilateral and cross-border cooperation is needed to deal with certain solutions, but in areas such as protecting civil aviation, multilateral cooperation and a global regime are required.

Keyword(s): terrorist groups and activities; antiterrorism; combating terrorism; aviation; counterterrorism

Wise, Richard. "Bioterrorism: Thinking the Unthinkable," Lancet, 351, No. 9113, May 9, 1998, 1378.

The author argues that urban terrorism in the future might involve newer technologies, including biological weapons of mass destruction. He believes it is a grave mistake to assume that terrorists will not be able to develop chemical threats.

Keyword(s): technology; biological terrorism; CBRNC; chemical terrorism; future trends; chemical weapons of mass destruction; biological weapons of mass destruction

Zelicoff, Alan P. "Preparing for Biological Terrorism: First, Do No Harm," Politics and the Life Sciences, [London]. 15, September 1996, 235-36.

This article is a commentary on Jonathan B. Tucker's "Chemical/Biological Terrorism: Coping with a New Threat" (see Tucker, Jonathan B.). Alan Zelicoff maintains that the terrorist use of chemical weapons will become, or already is, outmoded because of the ready accessibility of equipment, technology, and minimal obfuscation required to produce biological weapons (BW). He asserts that Tucker presents accurate technical data with the exception of six points regarding weaponized biological materials. In addition, the writer compliments Tucker for what he did not nominate as effective short- or long-term policy options and examines his policy recommendations to see which make sense. Finally, Zelicoff contends that policy options to counter the BW terrorist threat are inherently restricted and that some may even exacerbate the problem by offering a false sense of security based on the inaccurate premise that doing something is synonymous with doing something meaningful.

Keyword(s): CBRNC; chemical weapons of mass destruction; biological weapons of mass destruction; counterterrorism; combating terrorism; chemical terrorism; biological terrorism

Zilinskas, Raymond A. "Aum Shinrikyo's Chemical/Biological Terrorism as a Paradigm?," Politics and the Life Sciences, [London], 15, September 1996, 237-39.

This article is a commentary on Jonathan B. Tucker's "Chemical/Biological Terrorism: Coping with a New Threat" (see Tucker, Jonathan B.). Raymond Zilinskas disagrees with Tucker's assumption that the use of a chemical weapon by Aum Shinrikyo in March 1995 will weaken a longstanding psychological taboo that had deterred terrorists from using chemical and biological weapons and will raise the specter of more such incidents in the future. Zilinskas argues that terrorist groups are liable to employ biological, but not chemical, weapons in the near future but that the resolution to do so or not most probably will be made without any reference to Aum Shrinrikyo. He outlines the practicality of biological and chemical weapons and the threat of biological terrorism. He concludes that because the threat of biological terrorism is growing, the United States should adopt the well-reasoned short- and long-term options set forth by Tucker.

Keyword(s): CBRNC; chemical weapons of mass destruction; biological weapons of mass destruction; chemical terrorism; biological terrorism; counterterrorism; combating terrorism; terrorist cults

## Latin America

Arostegui, Martin. "Fidel Castro's Deadly Secret," Insight on the News, 14, No. 26, July 20, 1998, 7, 34.

Cuban dictator Fidel Castro is devoting a lot of his destitute nation's budget to secretive biological- and chemical-weapons research. This raises the possibility that he will share his germ arsenal with terrorists.

Keyword(s): biological terrorism; CBRNC; biological weapons of mass destruction

Economist. "The Americas: Rest-Home for Revolutionaries," The Economist, 347, No. 8073, 36-37. More than 1,000 terrorists and militants remain in Nicaragua. Leftovers of Germany's Baader-Meinhof gang and Italy's Red Brigade as well as Basque separatists, Islamic fundamentalists, and Palestinian extremists reside there.

Keyword(s): terrorist groups and activities; terrorism (general)

Franklin, Jane. "The War against Cuba," CovertAction Quarterly, Fall 1998, 28-33.

This article examines terrorist activities against Cuba carried out by the U.S. Cuban exile community, a 1997 assassination attempt against Fidel Castro, and the use of chemical and biological weapons.

Keyword(s): terrorism; CBRNC; biological weapons of mass destruction; chemical weapons of mass destruction

Fujimori, Alberto. "Terror, Society, and Law: Peru's Struggle Against Violent Insurgency," Harvard International Review, 20, No. 4, Fall 1998, 58-61.

The author, who is president of Peru, points out that terrorist organizations in Peru have struggled for a decade to erode the democratic system and to generate the "revolutionary conditions" necessary for obtaining power. Simultaneously, the short-sightedness, inaction, and even indifference of the traditional political sectors have helped to foment conditions favorable to terrorism. Fujimori presents a general discussion of terrorism in Peru.

Keyword(s): terrorism; antiterrorism; combating terrorism; counterterrorism

Locke, Charles E. "Hostage Seizure in Peru: What Lessons for the Marine Security Guard?," Marine Corps Gazette, 82, No. 11, November 1998, 74-76.

Using the Tupac Amaru Revolutionary Movement's seizure of the Japanese Embassy in Lima, Peru, as a case study, the author presents five observations about hostage situations. The topics discussed include diplomatic and consular services, military readiness, and hostage negotiations.

Keyword(s): antiterrorism; combating terrorism; terrorism; counterterrorism


Panjabi, Ranee K. L. "Terror at the Emperor's Birthday Party: An Analysis of the Hostage-taking Incident at the Japanese Embassy in Lima, Peru," Dickinson Journal of International Law, 16, No. 3, Fall 1997, 1-148.

This lengthy article examines the December 1996 attack by Peruvian rebels of the Tupac Amaru Revolutionary Movement (MRTA), the violent liberation of the hostages by Peruvian elite forces four months later, and the national and international impact of the event.

Keyword(s): terrorist groups and activities; terrorism; combating terrorism; counterterrorism

## Middle East

"The CIA on Bin Laden," Foreign Report, [Surrey], no. 2510, August 27, 1998, 2-3. [Call Number: terrorism]

This article gives a brief summary of a CIA briefing document on the Saudi millionaire-terrorist Osama bin Laden. The CIA acknowledges the role of bin Laden in Afghanistan in the 1980s and notes that his organization, Al Qa'ida, consists of Islamic fighters from many nationalities who have fought with bin Laden or who are being trained as fighters. The document also notes that terrorism is a key component of Al Qa'ida's strategy and that bin Laden cites Quranic references to justify it.

Keyword(s): terrorist groups and activities

"The Enigma of Bin Laden," Gulf States Newsletter, 23, no. 295, August 21, 1998., 3.

In a brief essay on Osama bin Laden, the newsletter provides details of bin Laden's youth in Saudi Arabia, his role in the Afghanistan fighting in the 1980s, and his sojourns in Saudi Arabia, Sudan, and Afghanistan after 1989. It notes that bin Laden is not a scholar or ideological leader but that he poses a threat solely because of his wealth and predicts that he will remain a threat through financial and logistical support for Islamist opposition groups everywhere.

Keyword(s): terrorist groups and activities; terrorism; future trends

"A Deal Between Extremists," Foreign Report, [Surrey], no. 2508, August 13, 1998, 1-2.

This issue carries a short discussion about an alleged meeting in February 1998 between Osama bin Laden, the Saudi millionaire who supports terrorism, and a senior officer of Iran's Revolutionary Guards. They reportedly agreed to combine efforts to oppose the U.S. and to help Muslims in Bosnia and Kosovo. The article notes that the Revolutionary Guards are opposed to the current political leadership in Tehran, which has softened its opposition to the United States.

Keyword(s): terrorism; terrorist groups and activities

Anonymous. "Deliberating Weapons of Mass Destruction," Chemical and Engineering News, 76, No. 35, August 31, 1998, 1, 72.

It is widely believed in the West that Iran is developing capabilities to produce weapons of mass destruction (CBRNC). However, none of the researchers with whom Chemical and Engineering News spoke believes the Iranian government is trying to develop nuclear, biological, or chemical warfare agents. The article summarizes an interview with an Iranian government official.

Keyword(s): CBRNC; nuclear weapons of mass destruction; combating terrorism; antiterrorism; nuclear terrorism

Anonymous. "Countering Terrorism," Gulf States Newsletter, [West Sussex], 23, no. 597, October 19, 1998, 8-11.

This article focuses on the growing US preoccupation with international terrorism in the Middle East in the wake of the embassy bombings in August 1998. Although the US has a number of policy options with which to deal with foreign terrorists, including the military option, this article warns against treating terrorism as a security issue, as the US seems to be doing. Terrorist acts are political acts and exercises in psychological warfare; they are best dealt with by US policies that promote political pluralism and economic reform, at least in the Middle East. [lb]

Keyword(s): combating terrorism; counterterrorism; terrorist groups and activities

Anonymous. "Militants-Hamas: Hamas Weakened by Internal Conflicts," Middle East Reporter Weekly, 89, October 17, 1998, 14-15.

The article discusses assassinations of six key political and militant leaders of the Palestinian Resistance Movement (Hamas), mainly by Israeli agents, and reasons for the schism between Hamas and activists from the group Ezzedine Al-Qassam.

Keyword(s): terrorism

Anonymous. "Terrorism: Bin Laden Aims at U.S. as Well as Saudi Royalty," Middle East Reporter Weekly, 88, August 29, 1998, 9-11.

This article enumerates the demands of Osama Bin Laden to the Saudi royalty. It also discusses the problem of apprehending suspected terrorists and of the U.S. law banning assassinations as a political tool.

Keyword(s): terrorism; antiterrorism; counterterrorism; combating terrorism

Anonymous. "The Outlook for Africa and the Middle East," Security Management, 47, No. 6, 1998, 18.

The article discusses reports of the U.S. Department of State's Office of Threat Analysis on the Middle East and Sub-Saharan Africa. Iran continues to be involved in terrorism, while Iraq poses terrorist threats to an uncertain extent. Lebanon is still a country that one should not visit because of armed clashes and the terrorists' inclination to harass Americans. Egypt and Israel are relatively safe, although terrorist activities still lurk in those countries. Africa has become a crime-infested continent as a result of industrialization. Terrorist activities are also on the rise in Africa.

Keyword(s): terrorism; terrorist groups and activities; combating terrorism; antiterrorism

Applewhite, Larry, and Carl Dickins. "Coping with Terrorism: The OPM-SANG Experience," Military

Medicine, 162, No. 4, April 1997, 240-43.

After a terrorist car-bombing in front of the main office building housing the Office of the Program Manager, Saudi Arabian National Guard Modernization Program, a mental health team interviewed members of the building's military unit. This article presents the findings. The researchers found a distinct pattern of psychosocial disturbance affecting 52 of the individuals wounded, ranging from sleep disturbances, concern for their families' safety or for their own personal safety, hypervigilance in their daily activities, to sadness, depression, irritability, and guilt. The study underscores the value of incorporating critical incident debriefings and command consultation by mental health professionals into a comprehensive counterterrorism program.

Keyword(s): terrorism; counterterrorism; antiterrorism; combating terrorism


Beres, Louis Rene. "Israel, the 'Peace Process,' and Nuclear Terrorism: Recognizing the Linkages," Studies in Conflict and Terrorism, [London], 21, No. 1, January-March 1998, 59-86.

Assessments of the Oslo accords on Israel's security normally focus on the risks of war and conventional terrorism. Yet there are compelling reasons to believe that the so-called Peace Process might also increase the risk of weapons of mass destruction (CBRNC) terrorism,, including nuclear weapons. With this in mind, the article, cast in the form of a Memorandum to Israeli Prime Minister Benjamin Netanyahu, discusses a number of pertinent variables and hypotheses. Exploring both the strategic and the jurisprudential aspects of the Oslo accords, the article examines underlying Palestinian orientations to the Peace Process, the Palestinian concept of sacrifice, and the various forms that nuclear terrorism might take. The concluding section, based on comprehensive consideration of Palestine Liberation Organization (PLO) and Palestine Authority documents and speeches, identifies the Peace Process as part of a strategy of jihad that could enlarge the risk of nuclear terror against Israel.

Keyword(s): terrorism; weapons of mass destruction in urban areas; nuclear terrorism; CBRNC


Callies de Salies, Bruno. "Libye: Evolution favorable," Defense Nationale, [Paris], 54, April 1998, 130-45.

This article examines political and economic developments in Libya during the regime of Muammar el Qaddafi, limited reforms, the role of the military, and the Islamic opposition. It also discusses Libyan support for international terrorism, the 1992 United Nations economic embargo, and totalitarian government.

Keyword(s): terrorism

Dickey, Christopher, Gregory L. Vistica, and Russell Watson. "Saddam + Bin Laden?," Newsweek, January 11, 1999, 34-36.

Iraq's Saddam Hussein, who has a long record of supporting terrorism, is trying to rebuild his intelligence network overseas. These assets would allow him to establish a terrorism network. According to U.S. sources, he is reaching out to Islamic terrorists, including some who may be linked to Osama bin Laden. The authors discuss how an alliance of the United States' two worst enemies might form and what it would mean to America and the world.

Keyword(s): terrorism; terrorist groups and activities; CBRNC


Dunn, Michael Collins. "Usama Bin Laden: The Nature of the Challenge," Middle East Policy, 6, October 1998, 23-28.

The article argues that Osama Bin Laden is primarily a spokesman and financier with links to various Islamist insurgent movements, that he is not a tactical planner, and that efforts to block and seize his funds may be more effective than U.S. air attacks.

Keyword(s): terrorism; terrorist groups and activities; antiterrorism; counterterrorism; combating terrorism


Fairhall, D., R. Norton-Taylor, and T. Radford. "Saddam's Deadly Arsenal," The Guardian, [London], February 11, 1998, 15.

Iraq's biochemical weapons include anthrax, botulinum, racin, aflatoxin, clostridium perfringens, VX, Agent 15, and others. The technology and materials for producing chemical and biological (CB) weapons are easily available nowadays, and they are much easier to make than nuclear weapons. And the new science of genetic engineering may lead to even more virulent microbes and poisons. Effective delivery systems are more difficult. One problem is how to disperse the agent without the missile burning up on impact or on reentry to Earth's atmosphere. However, after the Gulf War it was found that Iraq had been experimenting with pilotless aircraft.

Keyword(s): technology; CBRNC; chemical weapons of mass destruction; biological weapons of mass destruction; chemical terrorism; biological terrorism


Gambill, Gary C. "The Balance of Terror: War by Other Means in the Contemporary Middle East," Journal of Palestine Studies, 28, Autumn 1998, 51-66.

The article defines terrorism as the attempt to alter the policies of a political actor through the use of violence against civilians. It also analyzes the use of terrorism on both sides in the April 1996 clash between Israel and Hizbullah in Lebanon.

Keyword(s): terrorism; combating terrorism; counterterrorism; antiterrorism

Kaplan, David E.. "Tracking Saddam's Network," <u>U.S. News and World Report</u>, 124, March 2, 1998, 41.

U.S. intelligence agencies were on high alert as war with Iraq appeared imminent at the time of this article's publication. According to Larry Johnson, who was deputy director of the Department of State's counterterrorism office during the Gulf War, a U.S. bombing campaign would almost certainly result in major acts of retaliation against America. The most probable scenarios included car bombs, assassinations, and hostage-taking. Those most at risk were "soft" targets, such as U.S. firms and executives overseas. In the United States itself, the Federal Bureau of Investigation was giving priority to investigations of suspected Iraqi agents, and the Immigration and Naturalization Service had given the bureau a list of several hundred Iraqi students in America.

Keyword(s): terrorism; antiterrorism; counterterrorism; combating terrorism

Karmon, Ely. ""Why Tehran Starts and Stops Terrorism"," <u>Middle East Quarterly</u>, 4, no. 4, December 1998, 35-44.

Karmon raises the question of why Iran's leaders continue to sponsor terrorism when the cost in terms of Iran's own economic well-being and internal stability is so high. Part of the answer lies in the ideology of the Islamic Revolution in its Iranian guise, but Karmon finds that the policies toward Iran of the leading European countries and the United States also appear to be a key determinant of Iranian-supported acts of terrorism abroad. He suggests that only a firm and resolute stand by Western powers acting in concert will deter future Iranian terrorist acts and strengthen the hand of the moderate Khatami regime.

Keyword(s): combating terrorism; future trends; terrorism

Katzman, Kenneth. ""American Successes"," <u>Middle East Quarterly</u>, 5, no. 4, December 1998, 45-51.

Katzman discusses instances of American successes in defeating or diminishing international terrorism and the policies employed to bring about those ends. Drawing upon examples involving Iran, Iraq, Syria, Libya, and Sudan, he finds a number of cases in which economic sanctions, investigations and court trials, various economic and political incentives, and even military strikes have proven effective policies in dealing with state-sponsored terrorism. He postulates that the same mixture of inducements and punishments may be effective against non-state sponsored terrorists such as Osama bin Laden.

Keyword(s): combating terrorism; counterterrorism; future trends

King, Llewellyn. "When Terrorism Goes High Tech, Can Peace Result?," <u>Defense Week</u>, September 14, 1998, 2.

The new reality is that technology is changing terrorism in a way that may make it so fearful that even countries that do not like each other will have to cooperate to control it. Technology is increasing the reach of terrorism, decreasing its predictability, and altering its weapons of choice. Ballistics are on the way out, and chemicals and biological agents are on the way in. Now every state, large and small, must worry about the surreptitious development at the state level of almost undetectable arsenals that are cheaply made, easily hidden, and extremely mobile.

Keyword(s): biological weapons of mass destruction; chemical weapons of mass destruction; CBRNC; terrorism; antiterrorism; technology; combating terrorism


Kozlow, Chris. "The Bombing of Khobar Towers: Who Did It, and Who Funded It," Jane's Intelligence Review, [London], 9, No. 12, December 1997, 555-58.

The article provides a detailed examination of the bombing of the al-Khobar Towers, which housed U.S. military personnel, near Dhahran, Saudi Arabia, on June 25, 1996. The author states that the bombing was sponsored by an international network heavily supported by Osama bin Laden and tightly controlled by Iran. The article discusses the various stages of the operation, from recruitment and reconnaissance to smuggling of explosives and assembly of the bomb. Finally, the article discusses the various claims of responsibility.

Keyword(s): infrastructure protection; antiterrorism; terrorism; combating terrorism


Lewis, Bernard. "License to Kill: Usama bin Ladin's Declaration of Jihad," Foreign Affairs, 77, No. 6, November/December 1998, 14-19.

In its February 23, 1998, issue, Al-Quds al-Arabi, an Arabic newspaper published in London, provides the full text of a Declaration of the World Islamic Front for Jihad against the Jews and the Crusaders. The paper reported that the manifesto was faxed to them under the signatures of Usama bin Ladin, the exiled Saudi financier and alleged mastermind of the August 1998 bombings of the U.S. embassies in Kenya and Tanzania, and the leaders of militant Islamic groups in Egypt, Pakistan, and Bangladesh. The statement criticizes U.S. involvement in three key areas--Arabia, Iraq, and Jerusalem--and calls for violent resistance on the part of Muslims. Most Americans would regard the declaration as a gross distortion of the United States presence in Arabia. For many Muslims, the declaration would be regarded as an equally grotesque travesty of the nature of Islam and even of its doctrine of jihad, or holy war.

Keyword(s): terrorism; terrorist cults; terrorist groups and activities; ad hoc and transient terrorist groups


Mann, Paul. "Iraq Threat Spurs Push to Curb WMD," Aviation Week and Space Technology, 14, No. 6, February 9, 1998, 29.

Heads of state and civilian leaders from 46 countries have signed a declaration calling for urgent steps to prevent weapons of mass destruction (CBRNC) from falling into the hands of terrorists, loosely knit rogue groups, and outlaw states. Citing the immediate danger of Iraq's CBRNC, 117 present and previous leaders appealed last week for prompt and continuing steps to prevent further proliferation and to reduce existing stockpiles.

Keyword(s): CBRNC; antiterrorism; combating terrorism

Miller, John. ""Usama bin Ladin: 'American Soldiers Are Paper Tigers'"," <u>Middle East Quarterly</u>, 5, no. 4, December 1998, 73-79.

In a somewhat rambling and unfocused interview, bin Laden states his convictions and motivations and gives his views of the Saudi government, Russians, and Americans. He labels Americans as the world's leading terrorists and says they must be driven out of the Muslim Middle East.

Keyword(s): terrorism; terrorist groups and activities; combating terrorism

Miller, Judith, and William J. Broad. "Bio-Weapons in Mind, Iranians Lure Needy Ex-Soviet Scientists," <u>New York Times</u>, December 8, 1998, A1, A12.

Iran is recruiting former Soviet scientists who once worked in laboratories tied to Moscow's vast germ warfare program. Although most of these entreaties reportedly have been rebuffed, at least five former Soviet scientists have gone to work in Iran in recent years. Many more Russian scientists have disclosed such contacts and believe that Iran is developing a germ arsenal. This feature article also includes a photo of a Russian germ warfare scientist, a photo of the former Soviet germ warfare plant in Stepnogorsk, Kazakhstan, and a map indicating germ warfare institutes in the Moscow region.

Keyword(s): CBRNC; biological weapons of mass destruction; biological terrorism

O'Ballance, Edgar. <u>Islamic Fundamentalist Terrorism, 1979-95: The Iranian Connection</u>. London: Macmillan, 1997.

The book examines the role of Iran in various acts of international terrorism, including bombings at Israeli embassies and New York City's World Trade Center, airline hijackings, and insurrection in Algeria and Egypt. It provides some focus on the role of the Ayatollah Khomeini.

Keyword(s): terrorism; aviation; CBRNC

Ostrovsky, Victor. "Crash of Cargo Plane in Holland Revealed Existence of Israeli Chemical and Biological Weapons Plant," <u>The Washington Report on Middle East Affairs</u>, 17, No. 8, December 1998, 19-20.

Victor Ostrovsky, a former case officer with Mossad, the Israeli intelligence agency, discusses the exposure of chemical and biological agents on an El Al flight that crashed in Holland in October 1992. The agents had been purchased in the United States and were bound for Nes Zionna, a heretofore highly secretive military research facility that manufactures biological and chemical weapons located south of Tel Aviv.

Keyword(s): biological weapons of mass destruction; chemical weapons of mass destruction

Peleg, Samuel. "They Shoot Prime Ministers, Too, Don't They? Religious Violence in Israel: Premises, Dynamics and Prospects," Studies in Conflict and Terrorism, [London], 20, No. 3, July-September 1997, 227-47.

This article examines conditions and circumstances that enabled the assassination of Yitzhak Rabin, prime minister of Israel. It notes that these conditions present a counterculture of Messianism at the core of religious Zionism, which has matured into a formidable force waiting to erupt. Drawing on insights from studies of political violence in general and religiously motivated violence in particular, the article concludes that a violence tendency tandem fosters and encourages religious violence in Israel, from the vigilante activities of the settlers' Gush Emunim to the assassination of Rabin.

Keyword(s): terrorist groups and activities; terrorism; terrorist cults

Prunckun, Jr., Henry Walter, and Philip B. Mohr. "Military Deterrence of International Terrorism: An Evaluation of Operation El Dorado Canyon," Studies in Conflict and Terrorism, [London], 20, No. 3, July-September 1997, 267-80.

This study addresses the question of whether Operation El Dorado Canyon, the U.S. air raid on Libya in April 1986, influenced the pattern of international terrorism in the period that followed. Specifically, the study documents the frequency and severity of acts of international terrorism over a 41-month period centered on the date of the raid. Findings indicate that the level of activity of Libyan-associated terrorist groups and, after a brief upsurge, the frequency of attacks against U.S. targets both declined after the raid. Whereas the number of acts of international terrorism worldwide was similar for the periods before and after the operation, the postraid period was characterized by a shift from acts of medium and high severity to acts of low severity in violence. Although findings are inconclusive, they are consistent with the view that the raid had a generalized deterrent effect on international terrorism for the period examined.

Keyword(s): combating terrorism; counterterrorism; terrorism

Prunckun, Jr., Henry Walter. Operation El Dorado Canyon: A Military Solution to the Law Enforcement Problem of Terrorism: A Quantitative Analysis (Libya). University of South Australia, 1995.

This study, a master's thesis, evaluates the effectiveness of Operation El Dorado Canyon--the April 14-15, 1986, U.S. air raid on Tripoli, Libya. The raid was in retaliation for what the United States claimed was Colonel Qaddafi's sponsorship of international terrorism. The Reagan administration's decision to bomb Libya was based on the military doctrine of deterrence, a strategy employed to contain state aggression through the fear of retaliation. Previously, counterterrorism strategies were the sole domain of police and security agencies. Therefore, the air raid was the first time America used a military solution to what had been seen as a law-enforcement approach. Using quasi-experimental time-series analyses to test hypotheses relating to four outcomes of the attack, the study concludes that there was a strong correlation between Operation El Dorado Canyon and the change (reduction) in various patterns of terrorism after the bombing.

Keyword(s): combating terrorism; counterterrorism; terrorism

Ranstorp, Magnus. "Interpreting the Broader Context and Meaning of Bin-Laden's Fatwa," Studies in Conflict and Terrorism, 21, No. 5, September-October 1998, 321-30.

This article examines the "inner logic" of the fatwa issued by Osama bin Laden and a coalition of four other Islamic movements on February 22, 1998. The article first discusses the significance of the "bin Laden phenomenon" on terrorism in general. It then analyzes the underlying reasons and broader context of bin Laden's worldview and the fatwa's appeal to his followers for violent action. It argues that this fatwa, when combined with the content of bin Laden's "Declaration of War" in 1996, is neither revolutionary nor unique to broader Muslim concerns but rather is part and parcel of a broader contest over sacred authority in Saudi Arabia and over the continued U.S. military presence on the Arabian peninsula. The article explores these issues, as well as the way in which the fatwa illuminates crucial factors behind behavior of bin Laden and other Islamic revolutionaries.

Keyword(s): terrorism; terrorist groups and activities; terrorist cults

Risen, James. "A Much-Shunned Terrorist Is Said to Find Haven in Iraq," New York Times, 148, No. 51,415, January 27, 1999, A1, A6.

Abu Nidal, one of the world's most infamous terrorists, reportedly moved to Baghdad in late 1998 and obtained the protection of President Saddam Hussein. This development raises questions about whether Iraq is seeking to establish a terrorism network. Counterterrorism experts in the Middle East say that Abu Nidal remains a significant threat. The article reviews Abu Nidal's past associations with Iraq, Syria, and Libya as well as his presence in Egypt.

Keyword(s): ad hoc terrorism; ad hoc and transient terrorist groups; terrorist groups and activities; terrorism

Roberts, Mark J. "Hardening Overseas Presence: Force Protection," Joint Force Quarterly, Winter 1996/97, 117-20.

The article outlines measures for deterring terrorist attacks on U.S. personnel and installations in foreign countries in light of the November 1995 bombing of Khobar Towers in Dhahran, Saudi Arabia.

Keyword(s): antiterrorism; combating terrorism; operation of manned checkpoints; vehicle barriers; vehicle inspection

Roy, Olivier. "Un fondamentalisme sunnite en panne de projet politique," Le Monde Diplomatique, [Paris], 45, October 1998, 8-9.

The article discusses the politically radical and ideologically conservative Sunni Muslim fundamentalist movement that has drawn adherents from the Middle East to bases in Afghanistan near the Pakistan border since the mid-1980s. Topics include the recruitment and coordinating activities of Osama Bin Laden, formerly a citizen of Saudi Arabia; the movement's enmity toward Shiite Muslims as well as Christians and Jews; involvement in terrorist attacks against the United States; the lack of any clearly defined policy other than imposition of Islamic law; and success of the similarly motivated Taliban group in gaining control of Afghanistan.

Keyword(s): terrorism; terrorist groups and activities; terrorist cults

"Terrorising the Americans," Gulf States Newsletter, [ ], 23, no. 593, August 24, 1998, 8-9.

This feature editorial discusses the American government's response to international terrorist attacks of the mid-1990s in the Middle East. It is critical of the Clinton administration's "fortress mentality" and its defensive response to terrorism. Instead, it advocates a pro-active, offensive response based on working closely with American allies to dilute militant Muslim discontent with the U.S. and on fundamental changes in American foreign policy in the Middle East.

Keyword(s): combating terrorism; terrorist groups and activities

United States. Congress. 104th, 2d Session. House. Committee on National Security. Terrorist Attack against United States Military Forces in Dhahran, Saudi Arabia: Hearing Held September 18, 1996. Washington, D.C.: GPO, Superintendent of Documents, 1997.

The hearing examines investigations into the June 26, 1996 bombing at Khobar Towers housing complex conducted by the Committee on National Security, the House of Representatives, and a Department of Defense task force.

Keyword(s): antiterrorism; protecting structures; combating terrorism

Venter, Al J.. "Iraqi Germ Warfare Specialist Exposed As Double Agent," The Middle East, No. 285, December 1998, 12-13.

The author discusses the recent arrest of the Iraqi germ specialist, Dr. Nassir al-Hindawi, a U.S.-trained microbiologist who gave Saddam Hussein his original ideas about the use of poison gas and germ warfare. He later initiated Iraq's biological warfare program at the Al Hakam complex. The author provides some insight into the workings of Iraq's chemical and biological weapons manufacturing and Iraqi efforts to keep the processes secret.

Keyword(s): biological weapons of mass destruction; chemical weapons of mass destruction

Venter, Al. "Iran Still Exporting Terrorism to Spread Its Islamic Vision," <u>Jane's Intelligence Review</u>, [London], 10, No. 11, November 1997, 511-16.

According to former Iranian president Abol Hassan Bani Sadr, there are currently 17 organizations in Tehran, located in different ministries, that are directly involved in terrorism in one form or another, most of it abroad. The article discusses some of the terrorist training bases in Iran that have been identified. It focuses on the terrorism support role of the Pasdaran organization in Iran and also examines the country's quest for the atomic bomb.

Keyword(s): nuclear terrorism; CBRNC; nuclear weapons of mass destruction; terrorist groups and activities; ad hoc terrorism

Venter, Al. "Bin Laden's Tripartite Pact," <u>Pointer: A Monthly</u> Supplement to Jane's Intelligence Review and Jane's <u>Sentinel</u>, [London], November 1998, 5.

U.S. federal authorities have released details of a tripartite pact between Iran, Sudan, and Usama bin Laden, including links between the former Saudi terrorist's Al Qaeda Islamic organization and Iran's Ayatolla Ali Khamenei. According to the U.S. assertion, Iran had entered into a formal "working agreement" with Bin Laden and the National Islamic Front of the Sudan to work against the United States, Israel, and the West. The brief article discusses Al Qaeda's ties to Iran and Sudan.

Keyword(s): terrorism; terrorist groups and activities; antiterrorism; combating terrorism; counterterrorism

Yusufzai, Rahimullah. ""Conversation with Terror"," <u>Time</u> <u>Magazine</u>, January 11, 1999, 38-39.

Yusufzai, a Pakistani reporter for Time, ABC, and the News of Pakistan, reports on an interview with Osama Bin Laden in Afghanistan on December 22, 1998. The interview covers Bin Laden's view of America in the Middle East and offers some insight into his thinking and his Islamic convictions. [lb]

Keyword(s): terrorist groups and activities; counterterrorism

**North America**

Ackerman, Robert K. "Sensor Development Races Biological Warfare Threat," Signal, 52, No. 4, December 1997, 34-40.

The government is accelerating work on biological warfare sensors and related information systems in order to respond to possible terrorist attacks or use of pathogens on the battlefield.

Keyword(s): technology; biological terrorism; CBRNC; biological agent detection; antiterrorism; combating terrorism; biological weapons of mass destruction


Allen, Robin Lee. "More Security Is the Price Terrorists Exact as Risks Mount in U.S. Operations Abroad," Nation's Restaurant News, 32, No. 38, September 21, 1998, 27.

The risks involved for United States-based companies operating in a global economy were made dramatically more apparent in August 1998 when terrorists bombed a Planet Hollywood restaurant in Cape Town, South Africa. The incident also drove home the necessity of considering whether businesses closely identified with the United States can provide the type of security needed to minimize the probability of such incidents happening. Internationally minded food service companies need to develop more extensive efforts on defensive strategies and intelligence gathering in coordination with professional security experts or government agencies.

Keyword(s): antiterrorism; combating terrorism; terrorism


Anderson, Terry. "Painful Lessons: Hostage-taking and US Foreign Policy," Harvard International Review, 20, No. 4, Fall 1998, 62-65.

Although profit has replaced politics as a motive for kidnaping, official U.S. policy toward hostage-taking has remained virtually the same since the 1970s. Over the past twenty years, officials have made both public and secret deals with terrorists in certain instances. At other times, they have refused to even contemplate any form of contact without the immediate and unconditional release of the American hostages. The author argues that the government has not always followed policy or principle in handling hostage situations. Convenience, geography, and especially politics have played more important roles. Still, the United States has learned several important lessons over the decades, and blunders of the past are less likely to happen today. Americans held overseas can expect much less attention from their government today than in the past.

Keyword(s): terrorism; antiterrorism; combating terrorism
Andryszewski, Tricia. The Militia Movement in America: Before and After Oklahoma City. Brookfield, Connecticut: Millbrook Press, 1997. [Call Number: HV6432.A55 1997]

The book documents cases of recent activity by militant right-wing groups in the United States, including terrorist conspiracy and actions. The changing U.S. social and political scene is detailed as a background to such activity, with documentation of the beliefs and individual actions of terrorists and the responses to them by government authorities.

Keyword(s): terrorism (general); terrorist groups and activities; future trends


Anonymous. "Product Profile: Security," Airport Business, 11, No. 1, November-December 1996, 33-34.

The article surveys recently developed or marketed security-related products for commercial airport use, including automated alarm and inspection systems, drug and explosives detectors, access control systems, and surveillance equipment. There are brief descriptions of the technical specifications, applications, and operation of each device.

Keyword(s): inspection of overseas containers; automatic portal inspection; operation of automatic checkpoints


Anonymous. "Product Profile: Security," Airport Business, 10, No. 1, November-December 1995, 9, 20.

The article lists recently developed or marketed security-related instruments for use in commercial airports, including drug detection, access control, surveillance, and identification systems. There is a brief description of the specifications, application, and operation of each device.

Keyword(s): inspection of overseas containers; automatic portal inspection; operation of automatic checkpoints


Anonymous. "Manchester X-rays with InVision," Airports International [London], 28, No. 2, March 1995, 11.

The article lists the testing and installation sites for the InVision CTX 5000 explosive detection systems for commercial airports, concentrating on Manchester Airport's recent installations. At Manchester the systems will enable 100 percent inspection of checked baggage. At time of publication the CTX 5000 was the only such system to have FAA approval.

Keyword(s): technology; antiterrorism; inspection of aircraft carry-on luggage; inspection of aircraft cargo containers


Anonymous. "The U.S. Security Services Market: "By 2002, the U.S. Private Security Services Industry Should Be Worth $35 Billion, After Growing At 8.5 percent/yr.","" Appliance, 55, No. 12, December 1998, 15.

The Freedonia Group, Inc. study "Private Security Services" predicts that the U.S. private security services market will grow 8.5 percent per year to $35 billion by 2002. The growth will be driven by the privatization of public safety operations and the outsourcing of proprietary security functions. The private security industry's growth has been supported by the continuing concern for violent and property crimes.

In addition, newer services such as consulting and data security have emerged because of the spread of less-common crimes, such as computer terrorism and hacking.

Keyword(s): cyberterrorism; information warfare; antiterrorism; combating terrorism

Anonymous. "Terror: The New Growth Industry," Canadian Business, 71, No. 16, October 9, 1998, 54.

Industrial terrorists are stalking an increasing number of Canadian companies, particularly those involved in animal testing, logging, gas drilling, mining, and industrial-style farming. John Thompson of the Mackenzie Institute, a nonprofit research center in Toronto that studies terrorism, reports that similar acts have become a global phenomenon.

Keyword(s): antiterrorism; combating terrorism; terrorism

Anonymous. "Internet Information Poses Security Risk," Chemistry and Industry, [London], No. 18, September 21, 1998, 720.

There are fears that the publication of information on the risks of chemical accidents could increase the risk of terrorist attacks. Under the Clean Air Act, the Environmental Protection Agency (EPA) intends to publish such information on the Internet, much to the concern of the Chemical Manufacturers Association (CMA). As an alternative, the CMA has proposed to make this information available only on paper and CD-ROM to local emergency planning committees.

Keyword(s): technology; CBRNC; chemical weapons of mass destruction; cyberterrorism

Anonymous. "Terrorism Experts Discuss Structural Design Challenges," Civil Engineering, 69, No. 1, January 1999, 18.

Terrorists have switched targets from individuals to industrial installations, commercial properties, and transportation infrastructure. As a result, engineers are being asked to design structures that are bombproof and secure. Norman Glover of the AEGIS Institute was among 130 experts from such fields as civil engineering, national security, and building management who met in Reston, Virginia, for the Terrorism and Sensitive Facilities workshop.

Keyword(s): technology; antiterrorism; combating terrorism; blast mitigation; protecting structures; infrastructure protection

Anonymous. "Countering Nuclear, Biological, and Chemical Terrorism," Environmental Manager, 9, No. 4, November 1997, 10-12.

Several federal agencies have launched a joint initiative aimed at enhancing state and local governments' ability to counter the threat of nuclear, biological, and chemical terrorism. Pursuant to the Defense Against Weapons of Mass Destruction Act, passed in 1996, a number of federal agencies are now working together to provide training and support to state and local emergency response agencies. The effort is being led by the Department of Defense, in cooperation with several other agencies, including the Environmental Protection Agency (EPA). One of the EPA's key concerns with respect to the Defense Against Weapons of Mass Destruction Act initiative is the need to avoid duplicating existing emergency preparedness and response programs. The EPA is trying to get the word out to all local emergency planning committees to make sure they are aware of the Defense Against Weapons of Mass Destruction Act and to encourage them to get directly involved, if they are not already.

Keyword(s): CBRNC; nuclear weapons of mass destruction; chemical weapons of mass destruction; biological weapons of mass destruction; biological terrorism; chemical terrorism; antiterrorism; combating terrorism; nuclear terrorism

Anonymous. "EPA to Study RMP Data-Access Security Concerns," Environmental Manager, 9, No. 1, August 1997, 7-9.

In June 1996, the Environmental Protection Agency (EPA) promulgated the chemical risk management rule pursuant to Section 112(r) of the Clean Air Act, which will require owners and operators of more than 66,000 facilities to develop written risk-management plans (RMPs) for the chemicals they use on-site. Facilities that submit RMPs will have to include off-site consequence analysis (OCA) data that details, among other things, what could happen in the event of a worst case release of chemicals at the facility. Information contained in the RMPs will be made available to the public via the Internet. Some stakeholders who have been working on the development of RMP submission guidelines worry that making certain OCA data available over the Internet may give crackpots and amateur terrorists just the information they need to strategically place bombs or other destructive devices where they would do the most harm. In an effort to find answers to some of the many outstanding questions, the EPA plans to study the RMP data security issue over the next few months.

Keyword(s): technology; chemical terrorism; CBRNC; antiterrorism; combating terrorism; chemical weapons of mass destruction

Anonymous. "Terrorist Acts Drop but May Be More Deadly," Facilities Design and Management, 16, No. 8, August 1997, 9.

The most recent Federal Bureau of Investigation (FBI) report analyzing 1995 domestic terrorism showed that terrorists are becoming smarter, opting for fewer attacks with more deadly results, and experimenting with more and more unconventional weapons, such as biological and chemical warfare.

Keyword(s): biological terrorism; chemical terrorism; CBRNC; chemical weapons of mass destruction;

combating terrorism; antiterrorism; biological weapons of mass destruction

Anonymous. Improving Civilian Medical Response to Chemical or Biological Terrorist Incidents--Interim Report on Current Capabilities. Washington, D.C.: National Academy Press, 1998.

The 1995 sarin nerve gas attack on Tokyo's subway system by an apocalyptic religious cult added a new dimension to plans for coping with terrorism. Traditional military approaches to battlefield detection of chemical and biological weapons and the protection and treatment of healthy young soldiers are not necessarily suitable or easily adapted for use by civilian health providers dealing with a heterogeneous population of casualties in an urban environment. For these reasons, the Institute of Medicine (IOM), aided by the U.S. Commission on Life Sciences (CLS), has been asked by the U.S. Department of Health and Human Services' Office of Emergency Preparedness(OEP) to: (1) collect and assess existing research, development, and technology information on detecting potential chemical and biological agents and protecting and treating both the targets of attack and health care providers, and (2) provide specific recommendations for priority research and development. The interim report provides a baseline against which to evaluate the utility of technology and research and development (R&D) programs. Assessment of this work and its applicability to coping with domestic terrorism will constitute the second half of this study and be the focus of the final report.

Keyword(s): CBRNC; chemical weapons of mass destruction; biological weapons of mass destruction; biological terrorism; chemical terrorism; biological agent detection; antiterrorism; combating terrorism; counterterrorism; first responders

Anonymous. "U.S. Department of Energy Finds Clues to Terrorists," InfoWorld, 19, No. 27, July 7, 1997, 62.

The U.S. Department of Energy, which concerns itself with nuclear terrorism, is using software from ThemeMedia to find relationships between unstructured data that have not been preclassified by programmers. The object is to find clues to terrorist activities by uncovering unexpected links between news reports. ThemeMedia's Spire product was developed for federal government spies by the Pacific Northwest National Laboratory but has been licensed to ThemeMedia for business use. The Spire software is based on a proprietary algorithm that scans documents for concepts rather than words.

Keyword(s): CBRNC; nuclear terrorism; antiterrorism; combating terrorism; cyberterrorism

Anonymous. "Crossing the Threshold: The Increasing Threat of Biochemical Terrorism Has Security Experts on High Alert," Intelligence Report, No. 85, Winter 1997, 7-9.

A microbiologist with neo-Nazi connections has provided the extremist underground with a detailed blueprint for waging biological terrorism. Larry Wayne Harris claims that his self-published Bacteriological Warfare: A Major Threat to North America is designed to help readers survive a biological attack. But the scope and depth of information in the book also make it an effective do-it-yourself manual for mass destruction through biological terrorism.

Keyword(s): technology; CBRNC; biological terrorism; chemical terrorism; chemical/biological attacks; chemical weapons of mass destruction; biological weapons of mass destruction

Anonymous. "Preparing for War: Militia Groups Gather Intelligence on Public Facilities," Intelligence Report, No. 86, Spring 1997, 8-9.

A national militia network has developed a comprehensive plan for spying on the military, law enforcement, and public utilities in the United States. The American Constitutional Militia Network (ACMN), a coalition of paramilitary organizations, distributed a document entitled "Intelligence Gathering Guidelines" to members in early February 1997. These far-flung groups communicate via fax, short-wave radio, and, increasingly, the Internet.

Keyword(s): terrorist groups and activities; antiterrorism; combating terrorism

Anonymous. "Emergency Teams and Guard Train for Chemical Attack," National Guard, 52, No. 10, October 1998, 14.

The National Guard and other emergency agencies participated in a chemical terrorism training exercise sponsored by the Office of Emergency Preparedness. The exercise was designed to prepare them to respond to terrorist threats. The article discusses military exercises, military reserves, terrorism, biological and chemical weapons, and emergency services.

Keyword(s): CBRNC; biological weapons of mass destruction; chemical weapons of mass destruction; chemical terrorism; antiterrorism; first responders; combating terrorism

Anonymous. "American People Apathetic about Nuclear Terrorism," Pew Research Center for the People and the Press, news release, 1996, whole issue.

The report describes the attitudes of the American people toward the possibility of terrorist attack on an American city by chemical, biological, or nuclear weapons, as determined by surveys. Quantifying responses by degrees of concern, the report concludes that the public generally is not greatly concerned about the possibility, although it does recognize it.

Keyword(s): nuclear terrorism; future trends; chemical terrorism; biological terrorism

Anonymous. "Anthrax Scare Highlights Chemical, Biological Threats," Security, 35, No. 4, April 1998, 34.

The arrest in Las Vegas of two men suspected of carrying a deadly form of anthrax is a further wake-up call in the United States to the threat of chemical and biological terrorism. In an interview, Stefan Leader of Eagle Research Group, Inc. and a consultant to the Department of Energy, discusses his views on the subject.

Keyword(s): CBRNC; chemical weapons of mass destruction; chemical terrorism; biological terrorism; combating terrorism; antiterrorism; biological weapons of mass destruction

Anonymous. "Designing Out Terrorism," Security, 34, No. 4, April 1997, 23-24.

In an interview, Norman J. Glover, chairman of the Architectural Engineering Division of the American Society of Civil Engineers Working Group on the Mitigation of the Effects of Terrorism, discussed how the group came about, the types of things the group believes will help reduce terrorist damage, and what building designers can expect to see as a result.

Keyword(s): building rescue and evacuation; infrastructure protection; protecting structures; building collapse; blast mitigation; antiterrorism; combating terrorism

Anonymous. "Fighting Back on Terrorism: How to Minimize Harm," Security, 34, No. 9, September 1997, 48-50.

Ronald Massa, president of Lorron Corporation, a Boston-based bomb defense consulting firm, specializes in post-incident analysis of bombing incidents. The University of Oklahoma contracted him to study the Murrah Federal Building bombing. His goal is to establish what the dimensions of risk and hazards are.

Keyword(s): combating terrorism; antiterrorism; blast mitigation; building collapse; building rescue and evacuation; improvised explosive device threat or analysis

Anonymous. "Terrorism, Theft Concern Prompt Barrier Popularity," Security, 35, No. 12, December 1998, 57.

Vehicle barriers are designed to stop unauthorized vehicles from entering or exiting a property. Delta Scientific is one of the leading manufacturers of barriers. In this article, Mike Murray, director of sales, talks to Security magazine about barrier trends and recent developments.

Keyword(s): antiterrorism; combating terrorism; technology; vehicle inspection; vehicle barriers

Anonymous. "What Americans Think: Nuclear Terrorism," Spectrum: The Journal of State Government,

71, No. 4, Fall 1998, 7.

A June 1998 poll conducted by the Cable News Network (CNN), the USA Today newspaper, and the Gallup polling agency revealed that 71 percent of Americans believe that countries will use nuclear weapons against each other by 2008. The results of the survey on nuclear terrorism are presented.

Keyword(s): terrorism; CBRNC; nuclear weapons of mass destruction


Anonymous. "Airline Safety and Security Articles: Symposium," Transportation Law Journal, 25, No. 2, Spring 1998, 115-243.

This publication contains some recommendations for a new legal and regulatory structure for the management of the offense of unlawful interference with civil aviation. Subjects discussed include safety in the all-cargo air carrier industry, the motivational psychology of terrorism against transportation systems and the implications for airline safety and transportation law, aviation security in general, and current and future trends in aviation security in the United States.

Keyword(s): aviation; inspection of aircraft cargo containers; future trends; antiterrorism; combating terrorism; inspection of aircraft passengers


Anselmo, Joseph C. "Surveillance Critical to Antiterrorist Thrust," Aviation Week and Space Technology, 145, No. 14, October 7, 1996, 63.

U.S. intelligence agencies have billions of dollars worth of sophisticated equipment at their disposal, but when it comes to thwarting terrorist attacks on aviation targets, human spies are still paramount. While overall U.S. spending on intelligence has declined substantially in the last decade, the nation has sharply boosted the resources that it devotes to human intelligence to combat terrorism. America's vaunted signals-intelligence assets aid in the detection of terrorists by intercepting telephone, computer, E-mail, and radio communications. However, intelligence community veterans say that it usually requires human spies to uncover a group's plans. Intelligence agencies appear to be rising to the task.

Keyword(s): technology; surveillance; antiterrorism; counterterrorism; combating terrorism


Arquilla, John and David Ronfeldt. The Advent of Netwar. Santa Monica, CA: Rand, 1996. [Call Number: U163.A77 1996]

The study describes a new form of conflict in the "information age," which will include "lower-intensity conflict at the societal end of the spectrum." The concept of Netwar includes a wide variety of operations other than war, one of which is terrorism and measures to oppose it. Discussed are the new structures of organizations that will use cyberspace to reach political, social, or military goals, with one section specifically devoted to cyberspace terrorism and "cybotage."

Keyword(s): technology; cyber terrorism; future trends; antiterrorism

Austin, Mike. "Federal Emergency Management Agency Role in Counterterrorism," Officer, 74, No. 4, May 1998, 31-34.

The author argues that the effective awareness, preparedness, and ability to respond to, and recover from, a terrorist incident requires coordinated efforts at all levels of government. The possibility that a terrorist incident might involve weapons of mass destruction is particularly troubling.

Keyword(s): antiterrorism; counterterrorism; CBRNC; combating terrorism

Ballard, James David. A Preliminary Study of Sabotage and Terrorism as Transportation Risk Factors Associated with the Proposed Yucca Mountain High-Level Nuclear Waste Facility. Carson City, Nevada: State of Nevada
Agency for Nuclear Projects, 1997. [Call Number: HV6432.B35 1997]

The report assesses the vulnerability of the Yucca Mountain disposal site to domestic terrorism, given the nature of the site's proposed security and the past activity levels of terrorists using explosive devices. Various scenarios are proposed, using known plans for the site and the technical parameters of projected nuclear materials storage. Also offered are substantial statistics about past incidents of domestic terrorism involving explosives and transportation. Likely results and prevention systems are discussed.

Keyword(s): nuclear terrorism; antiterrorism; future trends

Barnes, Eric. "Protecting Public Transportation from Terrorists," National Institute of Justice Journal, No. 235, March 1998, 17-24.

Metropolitan public transportation networks are enticing targets for terrorists because these networks carry large numbers of people in a concentrated, predictable geographic area on a routine basis, and also because they are highly accessible. The article discusses the federal response to protecting public transportation systems, international cooperation to combat terrorist acts, the Federal Bureau of Investigation's role in infrastructure protection, the role of the Technical Support Working Group, the National Institute of Justice's response to identified counterterrorism needs, and counterterrorism training. Supplemental charts highlight information on topics such as "Assessing Technology Needs to Combat Terrorism," "International Conference on Land Transportation Security Technology," and "Examples of Counterterrorism Technology."

Keyword(s): antiterrorism; biological terrorism; CBRNC; chemical weapons of mass destruction; biological weapons of mass destruction; combating terrorism; chemical terrorism

Baum, Chris. "Protecting Water Supply," Security, 35, No. 10, October 1998, 14-16.

The Metropolitan Water District of Southern California is responsible for ensuring delivery of 60 percent of the water supply for some 16 million people in the Los Angeles and southern California area. One of the world's largest water-treatment operations of its kind, the District faces the usual security concerns, including civil disorder and terrorism. Mobile communication vehicles equipped to go into damaged, vulnerable areas are vital to keeping the District running smoothly.

Keyword(s): antiterrorism; combating terrorism; terrorism

Begert, Matt. "Spotlight on...the Threat of Domestic Terrorism," Police Chief, 65, No. 11, November 1998, 36-40.

There are about 200 domestic terrorist groups in the United States capable of executing attacks against U.S. citizens. Law enforcement agencies must be properly trained in dealing with these terrorists and their actions.

Keyword(s): terrorist groups and activities; terrorism; antiterrorism; combating terrorism; counterterrorism

Bender, Bryan. "US Cyber-Defence Task Force Is Now Operational," Jane's Defence Weekly, [London], 31, No. 3, January 20, 1999, 4.

The Joint Task Force on Computer Network Defense (JTF-CND), the U.S. Department of Defense's first operational cyberdefense unit, became operational in January 1999. The JTF-CND will assist in forming a long-term strategy against the growing threat from information warfare. It will also be responsible for providing direct support, such as technical advice, to the military services and commanders in chief when cyberattacks are detected.

Keyword(s): cyberterrorism; antiterrorism; combating terrorism; information warfare; counterterrorism

Betts, Richard K. "The New Threat of Mass Destruction," Foreign Affairs, 77, January-February 1998, 26-41.

The article describes the background of international relations and U.S. policy that makes terrorist attacks using weapons of mass destruction (CBRNC) more likely than before in United States cities. Betts points out that government programs have not kept up with the possibilities that this situation presents as a foreign policy problem. He emphasizes the threat of biological weapons, assessing the current situation of international deterrence and the likelihood of WMD use in light of that situation.

Keyword(s): chemical terrorism; biological terrorism; nuclear terrorism

Boyce, John. "Analyzing Security Needs," Airport Business, 11, No. 2, January 1997, 8-9.

The article describes a directive from the White House Commission on Aviation Safety and Security, including the conduct of vulnerability assessments and the formulation of action plans at all commercial airports. Implementation is to begin at the 41 largest US airports. The article lists common vulnerabilities found in the initial assessments, notably in package handling and inspection. Also described are methodologies and attitudes of participating airports toward the imposition of new security procedures.

Keyword(s): aviation; antiterrorism


Boyce, Nell. "Bioterrorism Special Report: Nowhere to Hide," New Scientist, [London], 157, March 21, 1998, 4-5.

The article discusses the first simulated anthrax attack in New York City, under the Department of Defense's Domestic Preparedness Program. As part of this program, the U.S. Army's Chemical and Biological Defense Command (CBDC) is helping city and state governments to get ready for a terrorist onslaught. However, a handful of trained response teams and a cadre of knowledgeable senior officials are not enough. According to experts, the United States is hopelessly underprepared for a biological attack. No anthrax vaccine is available for civilian use, for example.

Keyword(s): CBRNC; biological weapons of mass destruction; biological terrorism; combating terrorism; antiterrorism


Bridgegan, Gaylord, Dan Chilcutt, B.H. Basehart, and Marvin Dickerson. "Contained Response: Environmental Emergency Planning," Risk Management, 44, No. 5, May 1997, 40-42.

Natural disasters and acts of terrorism have heightened awareness of the importance of emergency planning, and effective response plans are especially important for coping with environmental disasters. In fact, the United States mandates disaster plans. The Emergency Planning and Community Right-to-Know Act specifies a structure that the emergency plans must follow. Although these regulations mandate the need to establish recovery plans, organizations also must consider how to adapt their plans to meet their unique needs. For most, the first step will be to create a facility safety committee, which should include representatives from operating and senior management. An outline should be prepared to ensure that the disaster plan covers crisis planning, management, and communications.

Keyword(s): antiterrorism; combating terrorism; building rescue and evacuation; first responders; terrorism


Broder, John M. "President Steps Up War on New Terrorism," New York Times, January 23, 1999, A12.

President William Jefferson Clinton has proposed steps to defend against terrorism. These include creating 25 urban medical emergency teams to respond to germ weapons attacks and training a new Cyber Corps of computer specialists to detect and defeat intrusions into critical civilian and military computer networks. The plan devotes $2.8 billion to prepare for attacks with exotic weapons and to combat computer warfare threats. The White House is also requesting $87 million, a 23 percent increase over current spending, to improve the nation's public health surveillance system to better detect the outbreak of an epidemic and determine if it is an act of nature or of deliberate terror.

Keyword(s): cyberterrorism; first responders; antiterrorism; CBRNC; combating terrorism; technology; counterterrorism

Brown, Randy. "A Plague on Our Houses," Buildings, 9, No. 2, February 1998, 22.

Buildings professionals daily battle with a host of real and imagined biological threats: indoor air pollution, Legionnaire's disease, nosocomial infections, and sick-building syndrome. These same professionals, however, may soon find themselves on the vanguard of a larger battlefront--biological terrorism. The article presents some suggestions for combating this threat.

Keyword(s): technology; infrastructure protection; protecting structures; CBRNC; biological weapons of mass destruction; antiterrorism; combating terrorism; building rescue and evacuation

Buck, George. Preparing for Terrorism: An Emergency Services Guide. Albany, New York: Delmar, 1998. [Call Number: HV6432.B82 1998]

The book describes and prescribes procedures for dealing with terrorist acts, concentrating on large-scale use of weapons of mass destruction and nuclear-biological-chemical materials. Included are documentation of previous incidents and responses, background of terrorist mentality and behavior patterns, and planning guidelines for responses at various levels of authority. Also included is detailed information on substances, equipment, and forms of organization.

Keyword(s): first responders; biological terrorism; chemical terrorism

Center for Strategic and International Studies. Wild Atom: Nuclear Terrorism. Washington, D.C.: CSIS Press, 1998. [Call Number: HV6431.W547]

The book summarizes the simulation game Wild Atom, held by the CSIS Global Organized Crime Project's Nuclear Black Market Task Force. The game scenario was theft of plutonium and weapons-grade uranium from a Russian nuclear site and subsequent threats by the Hizbollah and Chechen guerrillas to mount nuclear attacks at various points. Based on the scenario, security faults are detected and analyzed, with recommendations for improvement.

Keyword(s): nuclear terrorism; antiterrorism; terrorist groups and activities

Chalk, Peter. "The Liberal Democratic Response to Terrorism," Terrorism and Political Violence [London], 7, No. 4, Winter 1995, 10-44.

The article discusses the fundamental tension between the personal liberties of a democratic society and the control measures that may become necessary to respond effectively to terrorism. The author examines the underlying assumptions of each side and how they conflict, then he proposes a model of counterterrorism consistent with "liberal democratic norms."

Keyword(s): counterterrorism; future trends


Cilluffo, Frank J., and Jack Thomas Tomarchio. "Responding to New Terrorist Threats," Orbis, 42, No. 3, Summer 1998, 439-51.

The article describes potential terrorist attacks using weapons of mass destruction (CBRNC) in the United States (which are called inevitable), and it suggests a methodology for responding, using National Guard and military reserves, including proposed roles of troops in CBRNC response scenario. Training and organization of an "elite civil defense force" based on these personnel are described.

Keyword(s): future trends; CBRNC; antiterrorism


Collin, Barry. "The Future of Cyberterrorism: The Physical and Virtual Worlds Converge," Crime and Justice International, 13, No. 2, March 1997, 14-18.

This article examines the future of cyberterrorism. After defining the term and citing specific instances of cyberterrorism, the article discusses who cyberterrorists are and the threats that they pose. Without discussing specific counter-cyberterrorism measures, the article contends that the only solution is the quick deployment of a counter-cyberterrorist. The article includes a cyberterrorism glossary containing seven terms.

Keyword(s): cyberterrorism; information warfare; antiterrorism; combating terrorism; counterterrorism


Congressional Research Service. Terrorism--Looking Ahead: Issues and Answers for Congress. Washington: GPO, 1996.

The proceedings of this seminar held for Congress discuss various elements of the changing terrorist threat in the United States. Part two suggests possible actions by Congress to ensure an improved U.S. response to the perceived threat

Keyword(s): future trends; antiterrorism


Conrad, Andree. "In the Land Where Quality Is a Matter of Life--or Death," Apparel Industry Magazine, 59, No. 4, April 1998, 4.

An editorial discusses the changing nature of biowarfare. The editorial focuses on the workers at TradeWinds Affirmative Industries. These workers sew garments that must be impenetrable to weapons-grade epidemics.

Keyword(s): technology; CBRNC; antiterrorism; combating terrorism; biological weapons of mass destruction

Cooper, Cathy. "Plant Risk Data on the Internet Could Identify Terrorist Targets," Chemical Engineering, 10, No. 5, May 1998, 43.

During the May 1998 to June 1999 period, risk-management plans for 66,000 U.S. facilities have to be filed with the U.S. Environmental Protection Agency (EPA), which in turn must make the information available to the public. However, the EPA's proposal to post risk-management plans, including worst-case scenario information, on the Internet has riled plant owners and federal agencies concerned with national security.

Keyword(s): cyberterrorism; infrastructure protection; antiterrorism; combating terrorism

Cooper, Mary H., Jamie S. Gorelick, and Donald M. Haines. "Combating Terrorism," CQ Researcher, 5, July 21, 1995, 633-56.

The multipart treatment of the subject surveys the present situation of terrorism and antiterrorism policy in the United States, assessing how far new counterterrorism steps should go in light of privacy rights. The discussion of the issues includes potential loosening of wiretap restrictions and a discussion of future trends. The issue includes a chronology and a bibliography.

Keyword(s): antiterrorism; future trends; intelligence; surveillance

Corn, David. "Profits and Proliferation: Privatizing the U.S. Enrichment Corporation," The Nation, 267, July 13, 1998, 23-24.

The Clinton administration is considering extending its privatization campaign to the U.S. Uranium Enrichment Corporation (USEC). This government-owned, independent company produces fuel for nuclear reactors and plays a critical role in the administration's efforts to purchase Russian uranium to prevent nuclear weapons proliferation. President Clinton's plan may not only cost U.S. taxpayers as much as $1.8 billion but could weaken the program intended to prevent extremist groups and nations from obtaining bomb-grade uranium.

Keyword(s): nuclear terrorism; CBRNC; antiterrorism; combating terrorism; nuclear weapons of mass destruction

Crelisten, Ronald D.. "Television and Terrorism: Implications for Crisis Management and Policy Making," Terrorism and Political Violence [London], 9, No. 4, Winter 1997, 8-32.

The article analyzes the effects of television and the media on public views of terrorism. It then analyzes the effects of those public views on society's ability to manage terrorism situations and on the discourse on those situations that is conducted by policy makers. This leads to an assessment of the readiness of authorities to deal with terrorist acts.

Keyword(s): antiterrorism; counterterrorism; future trends


Crenshaw, Martha. "Unintended Consequences: How Democracies Respond to Terrorism," Fletcher Forum of World Affairs, 21, Summer-Fall 1997, 153-66.

The article discusses possible and actual policies adopted by democratic societies in fighting and responding to terrorism, also assessing the real-world responses that have followed those policies. The author analyzes the mistakes that have been made and attempts to show why even the most careful antiterrorist policies of democratic governments may not produce the intended results.

Keyword(s): antiterrorism; terrorism (general); combating terrorism


Deitz, Dan. "Virtual SWAT Team to the Rescue," Mechanical Engineering, 119, No. 6, June 1997, 144. Preserving life and liberty in terrorism situations is a thankless job, but thanks to training that uses virtual reality, it no longer has to be an impossible one. Through such training, police officers may acquire decision-making skills that, until now, could be learned only in the heat of a crisis. The key is a set of simulation components that can be assembled like building blocks to support the just-in-time development of simulated training scenarios. VRaptor, from Sandia National Laboratories and Silicon Graphics Inc., enables any number of users, devices, and simulation modules to be networked to create a shared virtual world.

Keyword(s): antiterrorism; combating terrorism; counterterrorism


Duffy, James E., and Alan C. Brantley. "Militias: Initiating Contact," FBI Law Enforcement Bulletin, 66, July 1997, 22-26.

The article provides basic information about the motivations and threat levels of various types of militia movements in the United States. Included is a "Militia Threat Assessment Typology," which defines four categories of group, based on ideological positions, training and equipment, and likelihood to engage in criminal activity. Based on the typology, recommendations are made for law enforcement agencies' approaches to making contact with militias.

Keyword(s): terrorist groups and activities; terrorism (general); antiterrorism

Eland, Ivan. "Preserving Civil Liberties in an Age of Terrorism," Issues in Science and Technology, 15, No. 1, Fall 1998, 23-24.

The author argues that the key to stopping terrorists is to be found in foreign policy, not aggressive policing of citizens. Americans should not have to give up civil liberties in order to end terrorism.

Keyword(s): antiterrorism; combating terrorism; counterterrorism

Ember, Lois R. "FBI Takes Lead in Developing Counterterrorism Effort," Chemical and Engineering News, 74, No. 45, November 4, 1996, 10-16.

The Science and Technology Center of the Federal Bureau of Investigation (FBI) was part of the massive security arrangement for the 1996 summer Olympic Games. It was specifically created to fill a void, a weakness in the initial plans for a response to a chemical or biological terrorism event: rapid and accurate agent identification. Countering domestic terrorism has become the top national security priority. So the response model, with its strong analytical component, fills a national need. The nascent model is in the throes of being refined, formalized, and maybe eventually codified. In the meantime, Presidential Decision Directive 39 lays out in general terms U.S. policy on counterterrorism. Although it does not directly address the model, it does give the FBI lead responsibility for managing a crisis posed by a credible threat of deployment of a weapon of mass destruction.

Keyword(s): chemical, biological, nuclear agents; biological agent detection; antiterrorism; combating terrorism; counterterrorism; CBRNC; chemical weapons of mass destruction; biological weapons of mass destruction; chemical terrorism; biological terrorism

Ember, Lois. "DARPA Expands R&D on Biowarfare Defense Tools," Chemical and Engineering News, 7, No. 7, February 16, 1998, 7.

The Defense Advanced Research Projects Agency (DARPA) has announced several new contracts under its biological warfare defense program to develop real-time sensors and medical countermeasures.

Keyword(s): technology; terrorism; antiterrorism; combating terrorism; CBRNC; biological weapons of mass destruction; counterterrorism; biological agent detection; first responders

Ember, Lois. "U.S. Forces' Achilles' Heel," Chemical and Engineering News, 76, No. 34, August 24, 1998, 45-46.

American troops have been so poorly trained to fight on a battlefield contaminated by chemical or biological warfare agents that if Saddam Hussein had used these agents in the 1991 Persian Gulf conflict, U.S. soldiers would have been unable to carry out their designated missions, and casualties probably would have been high. The Pentagon's Office of the Director General recently surveyed 232 military units across the services and found that only 45 unit commanders on Navy surface ships were fully integrating chemical and biological defense into unit mission training.

Keyword(s): CBRNC; chemical weapons of mass destruction; antiterrorism; combating terrorism; counterterrorism; biological weapons of mass destruction

Emerson, Steven. "Terrorism in America: The Threat of Militant Islamic Fundamentalism." Pages 33-54 in The Future of Terrorism: Violence in the New Millennium. Harvey W. Kushner, ed. Thousand Oaks, CA: Sage Publications, 1998. [Call Number: HV6432.F87 1998]

The author examines the large number of radical Islamic groups in the United States and assesses the danger they pose to the United States from within. He finds that they are torn between two conflicting emotions--the desire to keep the United States as a safe haven for themselves and their international operations, and the desire to launch a jihad within the United States. When the rage of the fundamentalists exceeds their self-restraint, terrorism is likely to be carried out in the United States. [lb]

Keyword(s): terrorist groups and activities; future trends; terrorism (general)

Episcopo, Peter F., and Darrin L. Moor. "The Violent Gang and Terrorist Organizations File," FBI Law Enforcement Bulletin, 65, October 1996, 21-23.

The writers examine the Violent Gang and Terrorist Organizations File (VGTOF), which provides information that helps to identify gang and terrorist group members. The VGTOF consists of two major classifications: the Group Reference Capability, which provides information on terrorist groups and gangs, and the Group Member Capability, which identifies individual members. At present, the VGTOF contains entries for 45 groups and 180 individual members, figures that grow as familiarization with the system increases.

Keyword(s): terrorism; counterterrorism; terrorist groups and activities; terrorist cults; combating terrorism

Eppright, Charles T. ""Counterterrorism" and Conventional Military Force: The Relationship between Political Effect and Utility," Studies in Conflict and Terrorism, [London], 20, No. 4, October-December 1997, 333-44.

The author compares the U.S. national security strategy's vision for counterterrorism to the political realm in which conventional military forces and terrorists operate. He analyzes terrorist acts and state responses in order to demonstrate that they have differing political effects, which undermine the political utility of a conventional military counterterrorist response. The author also discusses terrorism's nebulous place within the levels of war to reveal another facet of terrorism's different relationship to the political realm. He concludes that terrorism's relationship between political effect and utility challenges the U.S. national security strategy's conclusion that conventional military force used in "punitive" or "counterterrorism" operations is an effective political response to terrorism.

Keyword(s): terrorism; combating terrorism; counterterrorism

Fabey, Michael. "Lessons in Anti-Terrorism," Traffic World, 255, No. 3, July 20, 1998, 29.

According to Stephen W. Brooks of the Treasury Department, there are probably going to be more terrorist attacks in the United States, and the attacks are likely to be more lethal and more high-tech. The tools available to terrorists are becoming more accessible and more sophisticated all the time.

Keyword(s): antiterrorism; combating terrorism; terrorism (general)


Falkenrath, Richard A. "Confronting Nuclear, Biological and Chemical Terrorism," Survival, [London], 40, No. 3, Autumn 1998, 43-65.

Although national security leaders had tended to downplay or disregard the possibility that weapons of mass destruction (CBRNC) might be used by a nonstate or transnational actor in a campaign of mass-destruction terrorism, a shift appears underway, evident particularly in the United States since the early 1990s. This article addresses one basic question: how serious is the threat of nuclear, biological, and chemical (NBC) terrorism to the national security of modern liberal democracies? More specifically, where should the responsibility for combating the threat of NBC terrorism lie within a country's national security priorities as it allocates resources for new capabilities, organizes its existing capabilities, and declares its policies and threat assessments to the public? The author makes four arguments: increased concern with the possibility of NBC terrorism is justified; NBC terrorism is a low-probability, high-consequence threat; the harm caused by even one successful act of NBC terrorism in a major city would be profound; and the likelihood of acts of NBC terrorism in the future is low, but it is rising.

Keyword(s): CBRNC; nuclear weapons of mass destruction; chemical weapons of mass destruction; nuclear terrorism; chemical terrorism; biological terrorism; first responders; future trends; weapons of mass destruction in urban areas; antiterrorism; combating terrorism; counterterrorism; biological weapons of mass destruction


Fischetti, Mark. "Defusing Airline Terrorism," MIT's Technology Review, 100, April 1997, 38-46.

A range of high-tech bomb detectors for U.S. airports is now being examined. Although the metal detectors currently installed in airports can detect guns, knives, and other metal weapons, they cannot find hidden explosives. In the aftermath of recent terrorist bombings, Congress suddenly appropriated $160 million on October 9, 1997, for the Federal Aviation Administration (FAA) to hurry the installation of more than 500 bomb-detection units of various kinds into airports for a year of testing. No fewer than ten detection systems are competing, from X-ray machines and magnetic-resonance imagers to chemical-vapor sniffers, but no single machine is both fast and accurate enough to fulfill the FAA's certification criteria. Furthermore, all the proposed systems are expensive, and they raise serious social concerns. The article discusses the various detection systems.

Keyword(s): technology; aviation security; inspection of aircraft cargo containers; inspection of carry-on luggage; inspection of aircraft passengers; combating terrorism; antiterrorism; counterterrorism

Fishbein, Rand H. "Pulsed Fast Neutron Analysis May Help Quench Terrorism," <u>Materials Evaluation,</u> 55, December 1997, 1330.

Pulsed fast neutron analysis (PFNA) could significantly improve the ability of customs inspectors to stem the flow of contraband materials. PFNA is a nonintrusive inspection system that can reveal the contents of any sealed container almost instantly. Tests have shown the technique can detect minute quantities of explosives, drugs, fuels, hazardous substances, weapons, nuclear material, chemicals, and propellents.

Keyword(s): technology; inspection of overseas containers; inspecting vehicles automatically; biological agent detection; antiterrorism; combating terrorism

Fleming, Robert S. "Assessing Organizational Vulnerability to Acts of Terrorism," <u>SAM Advanced Management Journal</u>, 63, No. 4, Autumn 1998, 27-32.

The use of violence to further political or social objectives, which is roughly how terrorism is defined by the U.S. Department of justice, is on the rise today and cannot be ignored by organizations. Using the model presented, organizations can analyze their vulnerability to terrorism and take appropriate steps to contain that risk. The areas that need to be evaluated are the threat of terrorism (including the form it may take), potential targets, environmental factors, organizational exposures, and organizational preparedness.

Keyword(s): combating terrorism; terrorism; antiterrorism

Foster, Andrea. "CMA Details Terrorist Threat," <u>Chemical Week</u>, 160, No. 16, April 29, 1998, 69.

A report commissioned by the Chemical Manufacturers' Association (CMA) and released in April 1998 warns that terrorists using computer technology pose an increasing threat to public safety.

Keyword(s): cyberterrorism; information assurance; antiterrorism; combating terrorism

Foster, Andrea. "CMA Seeks Third Party to Weigh Internet Risks," <u>Chemical Week</u>, 60, No. 34, September 16, 1998, 12.

The Chemical Manufacturers Association (CMA) is urging the Environmental Protection Agency (EPA) to seek advice from a neutral third party, following its failure to reach agreement with U.S. counterterrorism officials on its plan for making worst-case accident scenarios available online. Topics discussed include the chemical industry, industrial accidents, terrorism, electronic publishing, and environmental regulations.

Keyword(s): CBRNC; chemical weapons of mass destruction; antiterrorism; combating terrorism; cyberterrorism; chemical terrorism

Foster, Andrea. "EPA Heeds FBI Advice on RMPs," <u>Chemical Week</u>, 160, No. 24, June 24, 1998, 31.

Under pressure from Congress and U.S. counterterrorism officials, the Environmental Protection Agency (EPA) is working to modify its proposal to have industrial facilities put the consequences of worst-case accidents online.

Keyword(s): combating terrorism; counterterrorism; chemical terrorism; CBRNC; chemical weapons of mass destruction; antiterrorism

Fox, Jeffrey L. "Pathogen Patchwork Could Cultivate Noncompliance," Nature Biotechnology, 14, No. 8, August 14, 1996, 940-41.

The article discusses the proposed rules for shipping and handling within the United States of infectious disease agents and toxins with a high potential for use by terrorists as biological warfare agents. The proposed regulations contain several important, potentially burdensome, components, such as a requirement to register facilities dealing with potentially dangerous agents. There are also concerns over who will keep records and who will be responsible for meeting the reporting requirements.

Keyword(s): biological terrorism; CBRNC; biological weapons of mass destruction; biological agent detection

Friedman, Norman. "Launching Tomahawks at Terrorists: To What Effect?," United States Naval Institute: Proceedings, 124, No. 10, October 1998, 107-108.

The author argues that the U.S. Tomahawk cruise missile attacks on Afghanistan and Sudan on August 19, 1998, crystallize both the thinking behind current U.S. military development and its inherent weaknesses. Topics discussed include terrorism, military policy, military engagements, and military strategy.

Keyword(s): combating terrorism; counterterrorism; terrorism; technology; antiterrorism

Fulghum, David A. "Cyberwar Plans Trigger Intelligence Controversy," Aviation Week and Space Technology, 148, No.3, January 19, 1998, 52-54.

The tightest security is drawn around the tactics and technologies that would allow the United States to penetrate a foe's computers and either clandestinely read his communications or actively corrupt the system. U.S. national intelligence agencies and the military are at odds over what can be attacked in a computer war. The former want to listen without ever giving an indication that they can roam foreign computer networks at will, whereas the latter want to gather data for a while and then use it to attack those who might threaten the United States. To defense planners, it is illogical to keep such information from military operators who must organize and employ the capability. The article suggests that a new working relationship between the national intelligence agencies and the Pentagon is needed in order to allow information to be passed to warfighters fast enough to retain its tactical usefulness.

Keyword(s): cyberterrorism; information operations; information war; combating terrorism;

counterterrorism; antiterrorism


Fulghum, David. "New Weapons Slowed by Secrecy Clampdown," <u>Aviation Week and Space Technology</u>, 148, No. 3, January 19, 1998, 54-56.

The article discusses some of the many and diverse weapons secretly
under development by the United States, with the objective of conducting offensive computer warfare. According to defense officials, there are eight nations that offer substantial cyber threats to the United States. They estimate that it would take 10 people to adequately ward off a single attacker. Therefore, an active offense is crucial to self-preservation. U.S. officials are busy assembling a cyberwar order of battle by tracking those who appear to be training to attack computers and determining where the training is being done.

Keyword(s): technology; cyberterrorism; information warfare; information operations


Gallagher, Eugene V.. "God and Country: Revolution as a Religious Imperative on the Religious Right," <u>Terrorism and Political Violence [London]</u>, 9, No. 3, Autumn 1997, 63-79.

The article provides a detailed analysis of how religious precepts are used by the extreme right in the United States to justify terrorism and other actions. The article explores the development of "civil religions" containing myth and ritual that sanctions acts of resistance against the government.

Keyword(s): terrorist cults; terrorist groups and activities; terrorism (general)


Gazzini, Tarcisio. "Sanctions against Air Terrorism: Legal Obligations of States," <u>Research Institute for the Study of Conflict and Terrorism, Conflict Studies [London]</u>, No. 298, 1996, (whole issue).

The article outlines the history of terrorist acts against aviation and evaluates the actions taken in response to them on the level of international sanctions. It discusses in detail the workings and strong and weak points of a variety of international cooperative actions to prevent recurrence of terrorism against aviation, and it describes the legal obligations of nations in working to improve international aviation security.

Keyword(s): aviation; future trends; antiterrorism

General Accounting Office. "Combating Terrorism: Federal Agencies' Efforts to Implement National Policy and Strategy," Online access: http://www.gao.gov/, September 1997, [np].

Under the sponsorship of the National Security Council (NSC), various interagency groups have been formed to coordinate the efforts of more than 40 federal agencies that combat terrorism. The intelligence community has its own committee on terrorism. Key federal efforts to prevent and deter terrorist acts include gathering and sharing intelligence information on terrorist threats and keeping foreign terrorists and materials from entering the United States. Federal efforts to combat terrorist acts and to manage the consequences of these incidents include designating lead agencies for crisis response, establishing quick-reaction support teams or units, developing contingency plans, and conducting interagency training and exercises. For both crisis management and consequence management, federal efforts include special teams and units to deal with nuclear, biological, and chemical weapons. Federal agencies are also assessing the capabilities of state and local jurisdictions to respond immediately to and manage the consequences of domestic terrorist incidents involving weapons of mass destruction and provide them with training and assistance.

Keyword(s): CBRNC; antiterrorism; combating terrorism; counterterrorism

Gilmartin, Kevin M.. "The Lethal Triad: Understanding the Nature of Isolated Extremist Groups," FBI Law Enforcement Bulletin, 65, September 1996, 1-5.

The article analyzes the psychological and ideological bases of terrorist and other extremist groups in the United States. The "lethal triad" of necessary elements includes isolation, projection of responsibility elsewhere, and pathological anger, each of which is described by source and role in the group's self-image. Based on these characteristics, the article recommends negotiating strategies for law enforcement agencies.

Keyword(s): terrorist groups and activities; terrorism (general); antiterrorism

Gozani, T. "Neutron-Based Nonintrusive Inspection Techniques," Proceedings of the SPIE [International Society for Optical Engineering], 2867, 1997, 174-81.

Nonintrusive inspection of large objects such as trucks, seagoing shipping containers, air cargo containers, and pallets is gaining attention as a vital tool in combating terrorism, drug smuggling, and other violations of international and national transportation and customs laws. Neutrons are the preferred probing radiation when material specificity is required, which is most often the case. Great strides have been made in neutron-based inspection techniques. Fast and thermal neutrons, whether in steady state or in microsecond, or even nanosecond pulses are being employed to interrogate, at high speeds, for explosives, drugs, chemical agents, and nuclear and many other smuggled materials. The article compares existing neutron techniques and reports on their status.

Keyword(s): antiterrorism; inspection of overseas containers; combating terrorism; inspection of aircraft cargo containers; inspection of carry-on luggage; vehicle inspection; inspecting vehicles automatically

Gross, Neil. "Bio Warfare's New Recruits," Business Week, No. 3575, April 27, 1998, 69.

Siga Pharmaceuticals Inc. recently received an $800,000 grant from the Defense Advanced Research Projects Agency for vaccine development. Siga's technique involves attaching foreign proteins to harmless bacteria that normally inhabit the mucous membrane of the mouth and nasal passages--the primary gateways to infection.

Keyword(s): technology; biological agent detection; CBRNC; antiterrorism; combating terrorism; biological weapons of mass destruction

Gunby, Phil. "RAID Teams to Respond to Terrorism Threat," JAMA [Journal of the American Medical Association], 279, No.23,, June 17, 1998, 1855.

Some state National Guard and other military reserve members are forming Rapid Assessment and Initial Detection (RAID) teams for medical and other responses to possible urban terrorism. Concern about terrorists who might attack U.S. cities with weapons of mass destruction (CBRNC) has been expressed at several medical meetings. The plan to establish one RAID team in each of the 10 Federal Emergency Management Agency (FEMA) regions is to be phased in over the next five years, at an annual cost of $49 million. The RAID teams have the role of first-response decontamination, treatment, and evacuation of those exposed. The Department of Defense is establishing a "consequence management program integration office" to coordinate this response plan.

Keyword(s): combating terrorism; counterterrorism; building rescue and evacuation; CBRNC; biological weapons of mass destruction; biological agent detection; first responders; chemical terrorism; chemical weapons of mass destruction; biological terrorism; biological decontamination; chemical decontamination

Hahn, Robert W. "The Cost of Airport Security Measures," Consumers' Research, 80, July 1997, 15-19.

The article assesses the current trend toward installation of more security devices in airports, often, the author says, without careful analysis of the cost effectiveness of each security measure.

Keyword(s): technology; inspection of aircraft passengers; inspection of carry-on luggage; antiterrorism

Hall, Stephen S. "Science-Fiction Policy," Technology Review, 101, No. 6, November/December 1998, 92.

According to an account in the New York Times, the Clinton administration's contentious new policy on bioterrorism was partly inspired by a novel entitled "The Cobra Event". This book centers on a fictional virus that causes horrible deaths. Prompted by fear-mongering, the administration has petitioned for $300 million in the 1999 budget to start stockpiling antibiotics, increasing vaccine research, and training state and local authorities to handle a chemical or biological weapons attack.

Keyword(s): CBRNC; biological weapons of mass destruction; antiterrorism; combating terrorism;

chemical weapons of mass destruction

Hall, Steve. "Security at the World Bank," Security Management, 42, No. 12, December 1998, 77-82.

The World Bank's high-profile activities and location in Washington, D.C. can make it a target of public protests, demonstrations, and possibly even international terrorism. The bank is also vulnerable to the same problems as other organizations, including street crime, assaults, vandalism, and internal theft. To guard against these risks, the World Bank has installed a $9 million integrated electronic security system that includes electronic access control and alarms, closed-circuit television (CCTV) surveillance, and emergency intercoms. The system is controlled from a security operation center, where officers can view and tape camera images, monitor all access-control transactions, and respond to alarms within seconds. The article describes the system in detail.

Keyword(s): technology; antiterrorism; combating terrorism; protecting structures; surveillance; infrastructure protection

Hamm, Mark S.. "Terrorism, Hate Crime, and Antigovernment Violence: A Review of the Evidence." Pages 59-96 in The Future of Terrorism: Violence in the New Millennium. Harvey W. Kushner, ed. Thousand Oaks, CA: Sage Publications, 1998. [Call Number: HV6432.F67 1998]

The author examines the state of research pertaining to U.S. terrorism and considers the likelihood of more terror in years to come. He calls for a clearinghouse to identify and catalogue government and academic literature on domestic terrorism on a timely basis. He sees the potential for continued antigovernment violence, especially from the Right Wing, against judges and other law enforcement officials.

Keyword(s): combating terrorism; future trends

Hanson, David. "Terrorist Threats to Facilities Concern CMA," Chemical and Engineering News, 76, No. 37, September 14, 1998, 10.

A study conducted by the Chemical Manufacturers Association (CMA) by Aegis Research Corporation reveals that if the Environmental Protection Agency (EPA) uses the Internet to disseminate highly detailed worst-case accident scenarios submitted by the chemical industry, the risk of a terrorist attack on a facility would increase seven-fold. CMA president Frederick L. Webber says that the study emphasizes the importance of a plan that balances the need to make information available to the public with the need to protect people from terrorism. According to the study, current EPA proposals do not provide that balance.

Keyword(s): CBRNC; chemical weapons of mass destruction; combating terrorism; cyberterrorism; antiterrorism

Hazelwood, Ed. "FAA Considering Backup for GPS," Aviation Week and Space Technology, 148, February 2, 1998, 58-59.

After several years of advocating Global Positioning System (GPS) and satellite navigation as the sole system that will be required in the future for all means of aviation navigation, the Federal Aviation Administration (FAA) is now retreating from that belief and has started looking for a backup system. The shift in philosophy follows a presidential commission report that called for caution before the elimination of the current ground-based radio navigation system and precision approach systems. The President's Commission on Critical Infrastructure Protection strongly urged a backup system for GPS, pointing to the threat of terrorism to a single-point system and the need for a full investigation of the weaknesses of the GPS. A January 9 Joint Resources Council meeting decided that alternative backup systems for GPS would be examined.

Keyword(s): technology; aviation security; antiterrorism; combating terrorism

Hess, Glenn. "Analysis Confirms Terrorist Risk of Placing Haz Data on Internet," Chemical Market Reporter, 25, No. 11, September 14, 1998, 1, 56.

The Chemical Manufacturers' Association has released a study confirming earlier warnings that the Environmental Protection Agency's plan to use the Internet to disseminate highly sensitive information on hazardous chemicals at thousands of industrial facilities will significantly increase the risk of terrorist attacks in the United States.

Keyword(s): technology; antiterrorism; combating terrorism; CBRNC; chemical weapons of mass destruction; cyberterrorism

Hess, Glenn. "Internet Access to Hazard Data Opposed," Chemical Market Reporter, 254, No. 19, November 9, 1998, 5, 26.

Federal law enforcement and security agencies remain opposed to the Environmental Protection Agency's plan to make highly detailed and sensitive chemical hazard information available on the Internet, even with electronic "speed bumps" to partially limit broad access to the data. It is argued that the plan would give terrorists a blueprint for potential attacks on industrial facilities.

Keyword(s): technology; cyberterrorism; information warfare; combating terrorism; terrorism; antiterrorism

Hewish, Mark. "On Alert Against the Bio Agents: Tactical Biological-Agent Detection Approaches Reality," Jane's International Defense Review, [London], 31, No. 11, November 1998, 53-57.

The article discusses newly developed biotechnology-based pathogen-detection devices, primarily using immunoassay techniques, that can be held in the hand and produce rapid results. Future developments expected over the next five years, such as instruments exploiting technologies such as DNA/RNA amplification, 'gene chips,' and biosensors, should result in other easily operated devices. The article discusses these new technologies in detail.

Keyword(s): technology; combating terrorism; counterterrorism; CBRNC; biological weapons of mass destruction; biological agent detection; biological terrorism

Hewish, Mark. "Shadows on the Shoreline: Specialized Equipment for Naval Special Forces," Jane's International Defense Review, [London], 32, No. 1, January 1999, 38-44.

Special Operations Forces (SOFs) in the United States total more than 46,000 personnel (active and reserve). During 1997, they deployed to 144 countries around the world. The article discusses the specialized equipment used by naval SOFs.

Keyword(s): technology; antiterrorism; combating terrorism; counterterrorism

Hileman, Bette. "Balancing the Right to Know with Security Issues," Chemical and Engineering News, 76, No. 11, March 16, 1998, 26.

The recent proposal by the Environmental Protection Agency (EPA) for placing countrywide disaster data on the Internet may not include sufficient safeguards to prevent terrorist use. Under the EPA's proposal, risk-management plans would be on the Internet, but searches would be restricted, and a CD-ROM of all U.S. risk-management plans would be available solely to those who register with the EPA. However, although posting such information on the Internet would help officials to protect the population against chemical accidents and could motivate some plants to reduce the potential for chemical accidents to occur, it could also make it easier for terrorists to target those plants where accidents could cause the greatest havoc for the surrounding population.

Keyword(s): chemical terrorism; CBRNC; chemical weapons of mass destruction; combating terrorism; antiterrorism

Hobbs, Erika. "Taggants Become An Issue," Coal Age, 101, December 1996, 55.

The April 1996 Oklahoma City bombing has brought the fear of terrorism to the United States, causing victims to file lawsuits against explosives manufacturers and U.S. lawmakers to propose that taggants be added to explosives and that additives be used to desensitize ammonium nitrate. Taggants would allow investigators to trace the source of a bomb--from the product used to the manufacturers to the point of purchase. The proposed use of additives has provoked debate that is directed by the mining industry, the largest user of explosive materials in the country, and the explosives industry, both of which fear a type of chilling effect in an already tightly regulated industry. Moreover, explosives producers are worried about an increased product cost from taggant use, and suppliers are concerned about the legal consequences of the ability to trace bomb contents to the producer and the merchant. A federal lawsuit against ICI Explosives USA filed by four survivors of the 1996 bombing and the expected reduction in the use of explosives by the coal mining industry are discussed.

Keyword(s): technology; improvised explosive device threat or analysis; weapons technology; antiterrorism; combating terrorism

Hodgson, Karyn. "10 Years After Lockerbie," Airport Security, 35, No. 12, December 1998, 19-25.

Ten years ago, a bomb exploded on Pan Am Flight 103 over Lockerbie, Scotland. The event jump-started the airport security industry, which has undergone some dynamic changes since then. In the bomb-detection arena in particular, renewed public interest, federal research and development funds, and advances in computer technology have made today's systems better, faster, and more effective than was possible ten years ago. But there is still much to be done in terms of both development and deployment, particularly in the United States. If Lockerbie was a wake-up call, many people feel the United States hit the snooze button, until TWA Flight 800 crashed.

Keyword(s): technology; antiterrorism; combating terrorism; aviation; inspection of aircraft passengers; inspection of aircraft cargo containers; inspection of carry-on luggage

Holloway, H.C.; Norwood, A.E.; Fullerton, C.S.; Engel, C.C., Jr.; and Ursano, R.J. "The Threat of Biological Weapons: Prophylaxis and
Mitigation of Psychological and Social Consequences," Journal of the American Medical Association, 278, No. 5, August 1997, 425-27.

The microbial world is mysterious, threatening, and frightening to most people. The stressors associated with a biological terrorist attack could create high numbers of acute and potentially chronic psychiatric casualties who must be recognized, diagnosed, and treated to facilitate triage and medical care. Media communications, planning for quarantine and decontamination, and the role of community leaders are important to the mitigation of psychological consequences. Physicians will need to accurately diagnose anxiety, depression, bereavement, and organic brain syndromes to provide treatment, reassurance, and the relief of pain.

Keyword(s): first responders; CBRNC; biological weapons of mass destruction; biological terrorism; biological decontamination; antiterrorism; combating terrorism

Husseini, Sam, Arnold Barnett, and James Flynn. "The Endless Fuse of Terror," MIT's Technology Review, 100, August-September 1997, 7-8.

The article is a discussion of Mark Fischetti's "Defusing Airline Terrorism" (see Fischetti, Mark). Five discussions of the April 1997 article are presented. The issues discussed include the technical and cost issues associated with antiterrorism measures and the privacy and civil rights issues involved in passenger profiling.

Keyword(s): aviation security; inspection of aircraft cargo containers; inspection of carry-on luggage; inspection of aircraft passengers; counterterrorism; antiterrorism; combating terrorism

Ikle, Fred C. "An Argument for Homeland Defense," Washington Quarterly, 21, Spring 1998, 8-10.

The article discusses the issue of what is the most effective agency to take the lead in crisis management of a biological or nuclear attack. Ikle argues that the military should be used in place of law enforcement agencies, as is now the practice, as a response to the National Defense Panel's recommendations (1998) for homeland defense. g

Keyword(s): first responders; biological attacks; nuclear terrorism


Jain, Vinod. "Thwarting Terrorism with Technology," World and I, 11, November 1996, 149-55.

The article examines new systems to detect concealed explosives, including imaging technology, radio-wave scanning, vapor- or trace-detection systems ("sniffers"), and neutron analysis.

Keyword(s): technology; antiterrorism; combating terrorism; vehicle inspection; inspection of carry-on luggage; inspection of aircraft passengers; inspection of aircraft cargo containers


Johnson, Jeff. "FBI, DOE Labs Team Up to Fight Terrorism," Chemical and Engineering News, 76, No. 36, September 7, 1998, 14-15.

Seven Department of Energy (DOE) national laboratories will provide technological aid to the Federal Bureau of Investigation (FBI) as it steps up activities to fight terrorism. About $5 million has been earmarked for the counterterrorism research and development program this year. The article discusses the proposed cooperation and new crime-fighting devices, such as a portable chromatograph-mass spectrometer instrument to identify substances at a crime scene.

Keyword(s): antiterrorism; combating terrorism; counterterrorism


Kamin, Blair. "The Murrah Building's Replacement: In Search of a Secure Space," Architectural Record, June 1998, 39.

The article presents the design for the federal building in Oklahoma City to replace the Alfred P. Murrah Building. The new design is intended to make workers feel safer while still emphasizing the accessibility of government. However, although flying glass accounted for the majority of the survivors' injuries at the Murrah Building, glass will be used as the main facade material for the replacement building.

Keyword(s): blast mitigation; building collapse; infrastructure protection; protecting structures; combating terrorism; antiterrorism

Kaplan, David E. "Bomb-Sniffing Tests Provoke a Dogfight," U.S. News and World Report, 123, November 24, 1997, 42.

A dispute among federal agencies over who sets canine antiterrorism training standards could cost the taxpayer more than $1 million and hinder the fight against terrorism. Six federal agencies use bomb-sniffing dogs, with large programs operated by the Pentagon, the Federal Aviation Administration, and the Bureau of Alcohol, Tobacco, and Firearms (ATF). The dispute began in 1996, when antiterrorism legislation poured $16 million into the training of more than 100 new dogs. The Treasury Department requested that the ATF set government-wide standards for training these dogs, and, in September, the agency issued a standard calling for containers for explosives. Other agencies feel that testing in such an artificial environment will produce dogs that are actually less effective in the field. ATF officials claim such criticism is because of jealousy that their agency was appointed to set the standards.

Keyword(s): technology; inspection of overseas containers; combating terrorism; antiterrorism

Kaplan, Jeffrey. "Right Wing Violence in North America," Terrorism and Political Violence [London], 7, No. 1, Spring 1995, 44-95.

The article provides a detailed analysis and typology of right-wing terrorist groups in North America, including Ku Klux Klan groups, the anti-Semitic Christian Identity cult, neo-Nazi groups, cults with religious-like philosophies (called by the author Idiosyncratic Sectarians), and single-issue groups. For each, the author provides a brief history and summary of current beliefs and practices. The last section traces the history of violent acts by such groups in North America, on a well-documented background of social trends.

Keyword(s): terrorist groups and activities; terrorist cults

Keating, Michael. "Preparing for the Increasing Threat of Terrorism," Disaster Relief Journal, 10, No. 1, Winter 1997, 10-11.

The article provides some basic advice and recommendations for responding to bomb threats, telephone threats, other bomb attacks, and mail bombs. One conclusion is that it is particularly important to cultivate an attitude that each employee is responsible for the security of his or her area.

Keyword(s): antiterrorism; combating terrorism; first responders; counterterrorism

Kelly, Robert J. "Armed Prophets and Extremists--Islamic Fundamentalism." Pages 21-32 in The Future of Terrorism: Violence in the New Millennium. Harvey W. Kushner, ed. Thousand Oaks, CA: Sage Publications, 1998. [Call Number: HV6432.F87 1998]

The author discusses why Islamic fundamentalism, the major component of the "new terrorism" of the 1990s , constitutes a terrorist threat to the United States. He suggests that radical Islamists view the United States as the preeminent outside power in the Middle East and the embodiment of Western values, which they abhor. Inspired by fundamentalist movements across the Middle East, terrorists are more likely to strike today than ever before, and the United States is a prime target. [lb]

Keyword(s): terrorist groups and activities; future trends; terrorism (general)

Kushner, Harvey W.. "The New Terrorism." Pages 3-20 in The Future of Terrorism: Violence in the New Millennium. Harvey W. Kushner, ed. Thousand Oaks, CA: Sage Publications, 1998. [Call Number: HV6432.F87 1998]

Kushner discusses the emergence of a new breed of foreign terrorist threat to the United States. An older generation of terrorists were state-sponsored and organized into corporate-type organizations, such as the Palestine Liberation Organization. In the 1980s, new groups emerged that are difficult to identify, whose organization and membership is fluid, but whose members are highly motivated and strike with deadly consequences. Many of them are Middle Eastern Muslim groups. [lb]

Keyword(s): terrorist groups and activities; terrorism (general)


Kushner, Harvey W. Terrorism in America: A Structural Approach to Understanding the Terrorist Threat. Springfield, Illinois: Charles C. Thomas Publisher, Ltd., 1998. [Call Number: HV6432 .K87 1998]

A handy reference for criminal justice and security administration professionals, this book provides an encyclopedic study of terrorism in the United States. Chapter 1 focuses on the definition of terrorism, the history of terrorism in the United States, and today's terrorism. Chapter 2 covers international terrorism, distinguishing between the "old" and "new" terrorist threats. Chapter 3 examines domestic terrorism and extremist groups. Chapter 4 assesses terrorist groups of the future, with emphasis on freelancers and what law enforcement agencies can do to cope with this threat. Chapter 5 is a complete analysis of the domestic, international, and extremist organizations that are currently active. Chapter 6 is a chronological summary of terrorist and terrorist-related incidents in the United States. And chapter 7 provides the names and addresses of organizations to contact for information concerning terrorists and extremists. The book uses actual case examples, such as the Oklahoma City bombing, to illustrate the actions of specific groups and freelancers.

Keyword(s): terrorism; antiterrorism; combating terrorism


Larsen, Colonel Randall J., and Lieutenant Colonel Robert P. Kadlec. "Biological Warfare: A Silent Threat to America's Defense Transportation System," Strategic Review, 16, No. 2, Spring 1998, 5-10. [Call Number: U162. S76]

The authors discuss the potential threat of biological warfare to the American defense transportation system. Such warfare could be perpetrated by either terrorists or conventional military opponents during wartime. Military forces are normally prepared to deal with such a contingency, but the same is not true of the logistical surface transportation system manned by civilians. The authors call for military planners to give attention to the biological warfare threat to the civilian transportation network during wartime, the impact of which could reduce or neutralize the advantages of surprise attack or of technologically advanced weaponry. lb

Keyword(s): biological attacks; biological terrorism

Leader, Stefan H. "Terrorists Go for Broke," Security Management, 42, No. 4, April 1998, 73-79.

Three years after the bombing of the federal building in Oklahoma City, a review of domestic terrorist groups and right-wing extremists suggests that while frontal attacks on government properties remain a serious threat, indirect attacks on the government's financial stability are also a major concern. Indirect attacks are being mounted against U.S. financial institutions and systems using everything from pipe bombs and other traditional weapons to less conventional paper instruments of destruction, such as bogus checks. These acts are committed both to raise funds for their cause and to disrupt the establishment.

Keyword(s): cyberterrorism; terrorist groups and activities; antiterrorism; combating terrorism; terrorism


Leifer, John. "Apocalypse Ahead: Nuclear Terrorism," Washington Monthly, 29, No. 11, November 1997, 30-35.

Americans believe that the nuclear threat has disappeared. However, the possibility that a rogue state or terrorist organization will use weapons of mass destruction (CBRNC) has increased since the end of the Cold War. According to physicists and members of Congress and of the intelligence community, the threat is the result of the convergence of four key developments: the proliferation of knowledge about how to build CBRNC, the increasing amount of fissile material, the deterioration of the security systems around such material, and the changing face of international terrorism. The writer examines these developments and identifies a number of actions the U.S. government should take to prevent nuclear attacks.

Keyword(s): future trends; CBRNC; nuclear terrorism; antiterrorism; combating terrorism; nuclear weapons of mass destruction


Leopold, George. "Federal Plan for Cyber-Safeguards Comes Under Fire," Electronic Engineering Times, No. 1008, May 25, 1998, .

Critics are warning that the Federal Bureau of Investigation (FBI) and the Justice Department have won an interagency struggle for control of U.S. policy for protecting the nation's telecommunications, transportation, power, and other critical networks. These critics argue that the U.S. policy debate on cyber-security was conducted in secret, and that reactive law-enforcement agencies are taking the lead in creating a proactive response to cyber attacks. Hardliners favor creation of a National Infrastructure Protection Center staffed by FBI agents and Justice Department lawyers, whereas others argued for an Information Sharing and Analysis Center modeled after the Center for Disease Control in Atlanta.

Keyword(s): technology; information assurance; cyberterrorism; antiterrorism; combating terrorism


Lesce, Tony. Wide Open to Terrorism. Port Townsend, Washington: Loompanics, 1996. [Call Number: HV6432.L47 1996]

The book treats several forms of terrorism to which U.S. society is vulnerable, with background information on the psychology and methodology of terrorists and recommended countermeasures. In the treatment of specific types of terrorist activity there are general descriptions of conditions and strategies as well as case studies. Also included are chapters on the role of law enforcement and security measures. Bibliographies are included in each chapter.

Keyword(s): antiterrorism; biological terrorism; chemical terrorism; nuclear terrorism


Levin, Brian. "The Patriot Movement: Past, Present, and Future." Pages 97-131 in The Future of Terrorism: Violence in the New Millennium. Harvey W. Kushner, ed. Thousand Oaks, CA: Sage Publications, 1998. [Call Number: HV6432.F87 1998]

The author discusses the Patriot antigovernment movement in the United States, a newly formed broad coalition of previously autonomous and loosely related social and political ideologies. He examines the historical factors that have led to creation of the Patriot movement and its current characteristics and organizational components. He affirms that violence by a fringe group of Patriot extremists will continue in the U.S., most violence being directed against government targets.

Keyword(s): ad hoc and transient terrorist groups; combating terrorism; counterterrorism; future trends; terrorist groups and activities


Levitin, Howard. "Preparing for Terrorism: What Every Manager Needs to Know," Public Management, 80, No. 12, December 1998, 4-9.

The article discusses steps that city managers can take using their localities' current budgets and resources to plan for the contingency of a terrorist attack. Topics discussed include strategic planning.

Keyword(s): antiterrorism; combating terrorism; counterterrorism


Long, Janice. "Defanging Terrorist Bombs," Chemical and Engineering News, 76, No. 10, March 9, 1998, 4.

A National Research Council committee that examined ways to reduce the threat of terrorist bombings has concluded that currently there is no practical method to attach identification taggants to all explosive materials available in the United States, nor is there a realistic method to negate the explosive properties of ammonium nitrate fertilizer. Edward M. Arnett, cochairman of the committee, says that because there is so much explosive material around, the committee stressed the need to detect the explosive material itself rather than a taggant placed on it.

Keyword(s): technology; weapons technology; improvised explosive device threat or analysis; combating terrorism; antiterrorism


Lucier, James P. "We Are What We Eat--And That Makes the United States Vulnerable," Insight on the

News, 14, No. 42, November 16, 1998, 6.

The National Consortium for Genomic Resources Management and Services (GenCon) concluded a recent conference in Washington, D.C. by pointing out the extreme vulnerability of the U.S. food supply to accidental contamination or willful attack by terrorists. The article discusses the food supply, food contamination and poisoning, and terrorism.

Keyword(s): terrorism; antiterrorism; combating terrorism


Major, Peter B. "A Dogged Approach to Bomb Detection," Security Management, 40, No. 2, February 1996, 34-36.

Explosives-detection technology is making headway with regard to cost, speed, and capabilities. But one approach to the problem--the use of explosives-detection canines--remains an effective alternative for security professionals for certain applications. The article discusses the special, natural olfactory capabilities of dogs and the advantages of using them in various bomb-detection situations. Selection criteria and training are also examined. The article concludes that companies should consider these versatile, reliable animals as an efficient and cost-effective way to safeguard their personnel and property from explosives.

Keyword(s): technology; aviation security; inspection of aircraft cargo containers; inspection of carry-on luggage; inspection of aircraft passengers; antiterrorism; combating terrorism


Mann, Paul. "Clinton, Congress Act Against Terrorism," Aviation Week and Space Technology, 148, No. 22, June 1, 1998, 30-31.

The White House and lawmakers have authorized a pilot program that would enable the Federal Bureau of Investigation (FBI) to help federal, state, and local agencies to obtain the appropriate equipment and training to shore up domestic preparedness against terrorist attacks with nuclear, biological, or chemical weapons of mass destruction (CBRNC). The pilot problem is an attempt to bring some integration to the 43 federal departments, agencies, and bureaus responsible for dealing with CBRNC terrorism. The article discusses anti-CBRNC initiatives being undertaken by various departments and notes two new measures taken by the White House. The latter include the appointment of a national coordinator, Richard Clarke of the National Security Council, to improve the integration of federal efforts, and the issuance of Presidential Decision Directive 63 (PDD 63) to protect "critical infrastructures" from terrorist cyber assault.

Keyword(s): cyberterrorism; CBRNC; chemical weapons of mass destruction; biological weapons of mass destruction; chemical terrorism; biological terrorism; antiterrorism; combating terrorism; counterterrorism; nuclear terrorism


Mann, Paul. "Government/Industry Alliance Urged Against Cyber Threats," Aviation Week and Space Technology, 14, No. 2, July 13, 1998, 65-67.

President William Jefferson Clinton has set forth what security experts say is a landmark strategy to meet the threat of cyber and other unconventional terrorist attacks on the United States' computer systems and basic physical infrastructure, including defense, aviation, and telecommunications. The strategy is intended to create a government/industry alliance to fend off computer hackers and other forms of terrorist attack on the nation's economic underpinnings. Security experts support Clinton's strategic approach. They caution, however, that the success of the strategy, which is officially titled Presidential Decision Directive 63, will hinge on unparalleled public and private sector cooperation.

Keyword(s): technology; cyberterrorism; information warfare; combating terrorism; antiterrorism; counterterrorism

Mann, Paul. "Officials Grapple with 'Undeterrable' Terrorism," <u>Aviation Week and Space Technology</u>, 149, No. 2, July 13, 1998, 66-70.

U.S. security experts say two factors make hybrid terrorist warfare enormously difficult to prevent: the weakness of conventional deterrence, and public disbelief in the threat. According to Air Force Major General John P. Casciano, an undeterrable terrorist threat is an individual or a group that feels that it has nothing to lose. Therefore, there is nothing you can do to threaten them. They will act, no matter what you do. Regarding public skepticism and complacency about the threat, the psychology of denial, ignorance, and apathy is absolutely pervasive, asserted Amoretta M. Hoeber, who heads a consulting firm on chemical and biological warfare. Other terrorist threats were discussed at a symposium organized by the National Defense Industries Association.

Keyword(s): terrorism; CBRNC; chemical weapons of mass destruction; biological weapons of mass destruction; biological terrorism; chemical terrorism; combating terrorism; antiterrorism; counterterrorism

Mann, Paul. "Ranking Civilians Lack Nuclear Crisis Training," <u>Aviation Week and Space Technology</u>, 149, No. 2, July 13, 1998, 70-71.

High-ranking U.S. policy makers are apt to make serious mistakes handling a nuclear terrorism crisis because they lack the requisite knowledge and training, according to a new Center for Strategic and International Studies (CSIS) report. The article discusses the "Wild Atom" report.

Keyword(s): antiterrorism; counterterrorism; CBRNC; nuclear terrorism; combating terrorism

Mann, Paul. "White House Sheds Inertia on Germ War," <u>Aviation Week and Space Technology</u>, 148, No. 18, May 4, 1998, 36-37.

President Clinton and the National Security Council (NSC) are at last taking steps to harmonize the multitude of federal agencies responsible for countering terrorists' use of biological, chemical, and nuclear weapons of mass destruction (CBRNC). Under an impending presidential directive, the NSC would become the leading coordinator of federal anti-CBRNC efforts. The council would also work out a national strategy for guiding these efforts.

Keyword(s): chemical terrorism; nuclear terrorism; chemical weapons of mass destruction; biological terrorism; biological weapons of mass destruction; CBRNC; antiterrorism; combating terrorism; counterterrorism

Manwaring, Max G. "The Security of the Western Hemisphere: International Terrorism and Organized Crime," Institute for National Strategic Studies, Strategic Forum, No. 137, 1998, 1-4.

The article notes that new security measures and policies are called for in this new generation of international terrorist activities. In the Western Hemisphere, various coordination strategies are suggested, including military and nonmilitary organizations in individual nations, but the recommended best solution is organization of policy and responses through the Organization of American States.

Keyword(s): antiterrorism; information assurance/warfare/operations; combating terrorism

McGuckin, Frank, ed. Terrorism in the United States. New York: H.W. Wilson, 1997. [Call Number: HV6432.T45 1997]

This collection of newspaper and journal articles presents a variety of viewpoints and levels of information on the current state of terrorism and antiterrorist activity in the United States. The book is divided into four sections: The Culture and Politics of Terrorism, The Terrorist and Terrorist Action, The Effects of Terrorism, and Preventive Measures. The last section also evaluates the future of antiterrorist measures.

Keyword(s): terrorism; first responders; antiterrorism

McMahon, K. Scott. "High-Tech Investments Needed to Counter Smuggled Weapons," National Defense, 80, January 1996, 28-29.

The article discusses a perceived change in the preferred method of delivering an attack using weapons of mass destruction (CBRNC),from delivery from outside to smuggling into the country and subsequent detonation. Briefly described are possible types of CBRNC to be used and the type of technological steps needed to counteract them.

Keyword(s): CBRNC; future trends; antiterrorism

McVey, Philip M. Terrorism and Local Law Enforcement: A Multidimensional Challenge for the Twenty-First Century. Springfield, Illinois: Charles C. Thomas, 1997. [Call Number: HV6432.M39 1997]

The book urges a stronger role for local law enforcement in preference to federal paramilitary approaches. It provides extensive background on the development of domestic terrorism and projects future trends and scenarios, with descriptions of worldwide terrorist movements and their methodologies.

Keyword(s): antiterrorism, future trends, first responders

Mefford, Larry A.. "Canaries in Cages: Responding to Chemical/Biological Incidents," <u>FBI Law Enforcement</u> <u>Bulletin</u>, 65, August 1996, 20-25.

The article describes the current and prospective threats posed by chemical and biological attacks by terrorists, together with the responses required from law enforcement and emergency management agencies at all government levels. The article discusses in detail the statutory structures for investigation of such crimes and the issue of community relations in conducting such investigations.

Keyword(s): chemical terrorism; biological terrorism; first responders; antiterrorism; future trends

Mercier, Charles L., Jr. "Terrorists, Weapons of Mass Destruction, and the United States Army Reserves," <u>Parameters</u>, 27, Autumn 1997, 98-118.

The article describes the danger posed to the U.S. by terrorists using weapons of mass destruction and the capabilities of the Army Reserve system to deal with a situation caused by such an attack. Discussed are the weaknesses in the current system and ways in which they can be overcome.

Keyword(s): CBRNC; antiterrorism; first responders

Messmer, Ellen. "Feds Fine-Tune Infowar Plan," <u>Network World</u>, 15, No. 37, September 14, 1998, 8, 74.

The U.S. government is working on an early-warning command center designed to identify the start of an infowar, that is, a hostile attack on key information systems. The National Infrastructure Protection Center (NIPC) will be the central point for collecting and analyzing security incidents from the commercial world and the government. Such information could reveal patterns that indicate a coordinated attack is underway. The key to the NIPC's success will be getting cyberthreat information quickly and completely from those under attack. Because businesses consider cyberthreat information to be sensitive data, plans are being developed about how they can report network attacks without negative repercussions.

Keyword(s): information warfare; cyberterrorism; counterterrorism; antiterrorism; combating terrorism

Miller, Judith, and William J. Broad. "Clinton Describes Terrorism Threat for 21st Century," New York Times, January 22, 1999, A1, A9.

In a White House interview, President William Jefferson Clinton said that it is "highly likely" that a terrorist group will launch or threaten a germ or chemical attack on American soil within the next few years. He made the assertion as the White House disclosed that the administration planned to ask Congress for $2.8 billion in the next budget year to fight terrorists armed with such unconventional weapons as deadly germs, chemicals, and electronic devices.

Keyword(s): future trends; CBRNC; biological weapons of mass destruction; chemical weapons of mass destruction; counterterrorism; combating terrorism; information warfare; antiterrorism

Monroe, Linda. "'Invisible' Protection?," Buildings, 91, No. 2, February 1997, 10.

The $82.2 billion security industry is growing because of an increased concern over workplace security and fear of crime and terrorism. The author questions the effectiveness of security measures being implemented.

Keyword(s): infrastructure protection; protecting structures; blast mitigation; surveillance; antiterrorism; combating terrorism

Mullins, Wayman C. "United States Terrorist Organizations." Pages 169-236 in A Sourcebook on Domestic and International Terrorism: An Analysis of Issues, Organizations, Tactics, and Responses. 2d ed. Springfield, IL: Charles C. Thomas, 1997. [Call Number: HV6432.M86 1997]

This chapter presents a listing and an in-depth discussion of the organization and aims of terrorist organizations active in the United States. These are subdivided into Left Wing, Right Wing, and Special-Interest Terrorist groups. Included are tables listings such major groups as Far-Right extremist organizations, Ku Klux Klan groups, Skinhead organizations, and Militia groups in the United States as of 1996. [lb]

Keyword(s): terrorist groups and activities; ad hoc and transient terrorist groups

National Research Council. Airline Passenger Security Screening: New Technologies and Implementation Issues. Washington, D.C.: National Academy Press, 1996. [Call Number: TL725.3.S44A36 1996]

The report focuses on new technologies to screen airline passengers and detect "threat items." The general mode of operation of several screening instruments is described, with collateral issues such as invasion of privacy, operator training, efficiency, and health effects also discussed. The strengths and weaknesses of each method or system are pointed out, as are likely future advances in the field.

Keyword(s): future trends; inspection of aircraft passengers; antiterrorism

Neely, DeQuendre. "Bomb Detection Takes Off," Security Management, 42, No. 4, April 1998, 12.

Vice President Albert Gore announced during a recent visit to San Francisco International Airport that the proposed fiscal year 1999 federal budget includes a $100 million request for bomb detection and other equipment at the nation's busiest airports. This short article is concerned with airport safety management.

Keyword(s): technology; aviation; inspection of aircraft cargo containers; inspection of carry-on luggage; inspection of aircraft passengers; antiterrorism; technology; combating terrorism

Nielson, Eugene. "QuickMask: Respiratory Protective Escape Device," S.W.A.T., 16, No. 9, March 1998, 45-47, 49.

Ten percent of the first responders (135 individuals) to Aum Shinrikyo's sarin gas attack on the Tokyo subway on March 20, 1995, were injured as a result of direct or indirect exposure to the nerve agent. Had the sodium cyanide contained in the bomb that exploded in New York City's World Trade Center on February 26, 1993, vaporized and not burned, the gas would have resulted in thousands of deaths. In any chem/bio attack, the key to survival is immediate protection and rapid escape. A respiratory protective device is necessary to protect eyes and breathing. The article provides a detailed discussion of the Israeli-manufactured QuickMask, which is widely used by U.S. security agencies.

Keyword(s): technology; CBRNC; biological weapons of mass destruction; chemical weapons of mass destruction; chemical terrorism; biological terrorism; biological attacks; chemical attacks; chemical/biological attacks; biological agent detection; combating terrorism; antiterrorism

Noaker, Paula M. "Detecting Weapons of Terrorism," Laser Focus World [Optoelectronics World insert], 34, No. 11, November 1998, S17-S20.

Although the best weapons detectors at key facilities in the U.S. infrastructure remain members of the K-9 unit, their backup team increasingly includes an array of supersensitive optoelectronic detection devices. The article specifies several counterterrorist devices that are far superior to the conventional metal detectors currently in use. Three categories of detection devices are discussed.

Keyword(s): biological agent detection; CBRNC; chemical weapons of mass destruction; biological terrorism; chemical terrorism; biological weapons of mass destruction; counterterrorism; chemical, biological, nuclear agents; antiterrorism; combating terrorism; technology

Noaker, Paula M. "Optical Imaging Catches Bad Bugs," Laser Focus World [Optoelectronics World insert], 34, No. 11, November 1998, S19.

Chemical and biological weapons detection is becoming big business. A large share of the research is focusing on development of technologies to detect and characterize biological hazards in the field at the point of contamination. Visual inspection of aerosol particles may serve as a first-cut screening leading to other, even more sophisticated analytical methods. The Fourier transform is one of these methods discussed in some detail.

Keyword(s): biological agent detection; CBRNC; chemical weapons of mass destruction; biological weapons of mass destruction; counterterrorism; biological decontamination; chemical decontamination; combating terrorism; technology; antiterrorism

Nordwall, Bruce D. "Cyber Threats Place Infrastructure at Risk," Aviation Week and Space Technology, 146, June 30, 1997, 51.

Cyber threats are putting the U.S. infrastructure at risk. Potential sources of cyber threats include foreign nations, disgruntled persons, organized crime, and terrorists--both domestic and international. According to retired air force general Robert Marsh, head of the President's Commission on Critical Infrastructure Protection, 80 percent of unauthorized intrusions up until now were by "trusted" insiders, generally as a means to express their unhappiness. This type of person would be easy prey for a terrorist group or nation to recruit. The president's commission, established by executive order in July 1997, aims to recommend a strategy for protecting vital infrastructures, the incapacity or destruction of which would have a weakening effect on the defense or economic security of America.

Keyword(s): technology; cyberterrorism; antiterrorism; combating terrorism

O'Connell, Tim. "Alleged Airport System Flaw Raises Tempers, Questions," Security, 35, No. 3, March 1998, 9-12.

A sometimes bitter fight among security designers, installers, and users broke out weeks ago when data leaked to the news media suggested that some security systems at high security locations have a weakness. The alleged flaw would reportedly leave the security of airports and banks exposed to terrorism. The physical access-control system is from Receptors, the Torrance, California, manufacturer. Receptors responded by placing the break-in blame elsewhere.

Keyword(s): airport security; technology; antiterrorism; automatic portal inspection; inspection of carry-on luggage; inspection of aircraft passengers

O'Connell, Tim. "Security and Democracy: At What Price Freedom?," Security, 35, No. 9, September 1998, 11-20.

Since the shooting deaths of two Capitol Hill Police officers, lawmakers and security professionals have been calling into question elements of security and execution. According to a preliminary report, the metal detector at the Capitol's Document Door was tripped as the gunman proceeded through the entranceway, but the audible alarm was quickly canceled out in the reverberation of gunfire. The position of the magnetometer in relation to the overall facility and in respect to the positions of Capitol Police officers is questionable. Another issue concerns body armor. Previous incidents of violence have occurred at the Capitol. The recent shootings prompted revision of plans for a Capitol Visitors' Center, which would be built a block from the Capitol. Tourists would be screened for weapons before coming any closer.

Keyword(s): technology; antiterrorism; operation of manned checkpoints; combating terrorism


O'Mara, Deborah L. "Security Soars to New Heights," Security, 34, No. 9, September 1997, 20-26.

The World Trade Center in New York City is going to extraordinary lengths to minimize the potential of future terrorist acts, such as bombings, by installing one of the most innovative, state-of-the-art, and proactive integrated security solutions ever applied to a commercial structure. Since the bombing in February 1993, the Center has turned its efforts to making it harder to penetrate the facility, without making it a fortress. The Center has undertaken one of the most expensive security and intrusion detection system enhancements and upgrades ever. By 1998 the multiphase, $50 million program is expected to be complete. Many of the techniques verge on the futuristic.

Keyword(s): antiterrorism; combating terrorism; protecting structures; surveillance


Ott, James. "Sky Marshals Reduce Hijacking Threat," Aviation Week & Space Technology, 145, No. 25, December 16, 1996, 26-27. [Call Number: TL501.A8]

The article discusses the effect of plainclothes sky marshals posted on random flights to discourage hijacking. Also discussed are the general requirements for running effective security points, with emphasis not on technology but on the positive results of proper training of security personnel, the human factor. The article describes how the sky marshal program works, including training requirements and deployment. _

Keyword(s): aviation; antiterrorism; future trends


Ott, James. "Profiling to Boost Security, but Funding Still an Issue," Aviation Week and Space Technology, 146, No. 18, April 28, 1997, 42-43.

A system of passenger profiling is emerging as the critical centerpiece of a $9 billion U.S. aviation security program that bristles with innovation but still lacks funding. U.S. airlines have no clue as to how they are going to raise the anticipated $800 million a year to fund their role in security enhancement. The profiling system will enable the airlines to adopt measures to thwart all-but-suicidal terrorists. The system is based on information that identifies individuals, their employment, their frequent itineraries, and how they paid for tickets. An additional set of information on individuals who may be known criminals and terrorists could possibly be deployed in the system. As part of a strategy approved by the Federal Aviation Administration (FAA), airlines, and airports, passenger profiling acts like a turnkey technology that frees the security process to work efficiently.

Keyword(s): technology; aviation security; inspection of aircraft passengers; antiterrorism; combating terrorism

Palm, Daniel C.. "Truth in Tagganting," National Review, 48, September 16, 1996, S1.

The article describes and evaluates the use of taggants (special identifiers making control and pursuit possible) on explosive materials with potential for use in terrorist attacks. The comparison is made between the control of such materials and the control of firearms, which only results in interference with legitimate use and continued possession by criminals and terrorists. The concept is judged a failure that will encourage black markets in controlled materials as terrorists continue to fabricate bombs from basic materials.

Keyword(s): technology; antiterrorism; chemical terrorism; future trends

Pasternak, Douglas, and Bruce B. Auster. "Terrorism at the Touch of a Keyboard," U.S. News and World Report, 125, No. 2, July 13, 1998, 37.

CIA director George Tenet recently informed Congress that at least a dozen countries, some hostile to America, are developing programs to attack other countries' information and computer systems. To help industries protect themselves from both foreign and domestic hacker attacks, the government has established the National Infrastructure Protection Center, which will be staffed by 125 people from the Federal Bureau of Investigation, other agencies, and industry.

Keyword(s): cyberterrorism; information assurance; antiterrorism; counterterrorism; combating terrorism

Paula, Greg. "Crime-Fighting Sensors," Mechanical Engineering, 120, January 1998, 66-68.

A range of technologies are being developed that can sense ceramic weapons, plastic explosives, chemical weapons, and organic materials. These technologies would help protect citizens from terrorism and aid police in solving crimes. Sandia National Laboratories in Albuquerque, New Mexico, has developed an explosives-detection portal based on preconcentrator technology. The Rensselaer Polytechnic Institute in Troy, New York, has developed an imaging system to detect plastic explosives. In addition, Brookhaven National Laboratory in Upton, New York, has developed a sensor to detect chemical weapons.

Keyword(s): technology; biological agent detection; inspection of carry-on luggage; biological terrorism; CBRNC; antiterrorism; combating terrorism; chemical terrorism

Paulsgrove, Robin F. "It Can Happen Here," NFPA Journal, 90, March-April 1996, 35.

The first worldwide conference on fire and emergency response to terrorism was held at the end of 1995 as a result of the Oklahoma City bombing. The conference concentrated on preparing for, mitigating, and responding to terrorist events. Domestic and international case studies were presented, each focusing on the same theme: the need to develop a cooperative partnership with local law enforcement and emergency medical agencies, along with a coordinated incident command system, prior to a possible crisis.

Keyword(s): first responders; building rescue and evacuation; antiterrorism; combating terrorism

Perle, Richard N., and Stansfield Turner. International Terrorism. College Park, Maryland: University of Maryland, School of Public Affairs, and the Norman and Florence Brody Family Foundation, 1997.

In this edited transcript, Richard N. Perle, a former Department of Defense official, and Stansfield Turner, a former director of the Central Intelligence Agency (CIA), debate the question: Should the United States be more willing to use military force against international terrorists? Perle argues the positive, whereas Turner argues the negative. Interestingly enough, both speakers more or less agree that military action should not be ruled out. However, it should only be used when force is the best option.

Keyword(s): terrorism (general); combating terrorism; counterterrorism; antiterrorism

Peters, Katherine McIntire. "Deadly Strike," Government Executive, 29, No. 7, July 1997, 22-27.

The threat of biological and chemical weapons attacks by extremist groups hostile to the government is real. Biological and chemical weapons have long been considered the poor nation's nuclear weapon, because they are comparatively easy and cheap to develop and use, and can kill thousands. Federal Bureau of Investigation (FBI) Director Louis Freeh is so concerned about terrorism in the United States that he had tripled the bureau's counterterrorism force over the last three years, raising to 2,600 the number of FBI personnel dedicated to the effort. The Central Intelligence Agency has created a Terrorism Warning Group, whose sole mission is to make sure that civilian and military leaders are alerted to specific terrorist threats. The Federal Emergency Management Agency is heading up an interagency Domestic Preparedness Program to develop a coordinated federal response to terrorism and enhance state and local response capabilities.

Keyword(s): CBRNC; biological weapons of mass destruction; biological terrorism; chemical terrorism; combating terrorism; counterterrorism; antiterrorism; chemical weapons of mass destruction

Peters, Katherine McIntire. "DoD Hones Top Anti-Terrorist Weapon," Government Executive, 29, No. 4, April 1997, 42.

Training military personnel and their families to be aware of and react to terrorist activity will become a critical weapon in the Pentagon's antiterrorism arsenal. This brief article describes the four levels of a comprehensive training program being designed by Defense Department officials to raise the consciousness of employees and reduce the military's vulnerabilities to terrorism.

Keyword(s): antiterrorism; combating terrorism; counterterrorism

Phillips, Edward H. "Mix of Technologies Key To Increased Security," Aviation Week and Space Technology, 145, No. 15, October 7, 1996, 50-52.

Installing state-of-the-art bomb-detection equipment could significantly increase airport security, but even today's most advanced systems have limited capabilities, are expensive, and would require three to five years to deploy on a national scale. Many see technology as ultimately the best hope for staying one step ahead of terrorists. Without systems capable of performing noninvasive inspections of passengers and checked and carry-on baggage, however, delays at airports will escalate. Providing effective security against terrorism is a complex problem chiefly because of the size of the U.S. air transportation system, the great diversity among airlines and the airports they serve, and the unpredictable nature of terrorism. The Federal Aviation Administration (FAA) has 40 projects underway to develop improved explosive-detection equipment, 19 of which are new, prototype systems. The other 21 projects involve basic research or improving existing components used in such systems.

Keyword(s): technology; antiterrorism; combating terrorism; inspection of aircraft passengers; inspection of carry-on luggage; inspection of aircraft cargo containers; aviation security

Phillips, James, and James H. Anderson. "Countering International Terrorism," Heritage Foundation Policy Paper.

The article argues that the proliferation of weapons of mass destruction (CBRNC) has made the formulation of an effective counterterrorism policy a moral and strategic imperative. In a world awash with low-level violence, terrorists seeking to dramatize their causes will likely resort to CBRNC as a way to inflict mass casualties. The interconnected nature of the global economy has made the spread of these technologies increasingly difficult. The article examines the issues, the facts, and the record and makes recommendations for what to do in 1999.

Keyword(s): CBRNC; combating terrorism; antiterrorism; counterterrorism

Piper, George. "Corporate Threat: Seminar Highlights Security Considerations," Airport Business, 11, No. 1, November-December 1996, 18.

The article summarizes an airport security presentation at the Corporate Aviation Security and Preventative Behavior Seminar by Air Security International. The presentation described factors of pilot vulnerability and techniques that corporate pilots can use for threat evaluation. Also discussed are changes to the FAA's airport access standards.

Keyword(s): aviation; antiterrorism

Polilo, R., and W. Higbie. "Deploying Explosives Detection Systems at U.S. Airports," Journal of Air Traffic Control, 39, No. 2, April-June 1997, 40-43.

The aviation industry is an attractive target for terrorists because of its high profile and public nature. To mitigate the terrorist threat and further increase aviation security, the Federal Aviation Administration (FAA) has taken a proactive initiative of fast-track deployment of explosives detection systems (EDSs) and explosives detection devices (EDDs) at U.S. airports. The foremost challenge to the FAA airport operators, air carriers, and industry participants is the integration of EDDs and EDSs into airport systems while minimizing operational disruptions, containing costs, and meeting all regulatory standards. The article discusses the FAA's efforts in applying explosives-detection technology to the real-world airport environment. In short, the stage has been set for wide-scale installation of explosives-detection technology at airports throughout the United States.

Keyword(s): technology; aviation; inspection of aircraft cargo containers; inspection of carry-on luggage; inspection of aircraft passengers; antiterrorism; combating terrorism; counterterrorism; inspection of aircraft passengers

Porter, Patrick L., and Deborah Radcliff. "The CIA's Biggest Issue is Sharing App Information," Software Magazine, 17, No. 3, March 1997, 35-36.

The biggest challenge in bringing the Central Intelligence Agency's (CIA's) outdated code into Year 2000 compliance is tracking down some 3,000 mostly homegrown legacy applications (app) among hundreds of fragmented, departmentalized miniagencies, access to which is granted only on a need-to-know basis. The CIA, as well as its Crime and Narcotics Center and the Counter Terrorism Center, must share sensitive data with a dozen other law enforcement and national security organizations. To repair the Year 2000 problem, a 14-person Information Policy Board was formed, consisting of department and information systems (IS) managers. Reporting to Sherry Burns, the CIA's Year 2000 project director, are four IS managers in Administration, Intelligence, Operations, and Science/Technology. Each individual in the agency is responsible for any program he or she has built at the desktop. The agency is also conducting a search for Year 2000 consulting firms and evaluating Year 2000 tools it can use to conduct impact analysis, identify critical applications and potential code problems, and also generate code fixes in numerous languages.

Keyword(s): technology; information assurance; antiterrorism; counterterrorism; combating terrorism

Potomac Institute for Policy Studies. Conference on Countering Biological Terrorism: Strategic Firepower in the Hands of Many?. Arlington, Virginia: PIPS, 1998.

This collection of papers and discussions is essentially a transcription of the Potomac Institute for Policy Studies' conference on Biological Terrorism, held on August 12-13, 1998. A multitude of counter-bioterrorism issues are discussed. Included are explorations of detection procedures and technologies, the role of governmental agencies if an attack takes place, the role that private firms play in detection of and protection against biological warfare (BW), what new detection and defensive technologies are in development, and what sort of terrorist group would resort to BW. It also contains an interesting discussion of how religion impacts terrorist groups.

Keyword(s): CBRNC; biological weapons of mass destruction; biological terrorism; future trends; antiterrorism; combating terrorism

Prina, L. Edgar. "It Was Only a War Game," Sea Power, 41, No. 11, November 1998, 46-48.

One of the results of the November 19-20, 1996, "Wild Atom Nuclear Terrorism" exercise was the revelation that the United States is "singularly ill-prepared" to protect against a terrorist attack involving weapons of mass destruction. The article discusses the military exercise, military training, terrorism, nuclear weapons, biological and chemical weapons, military readiness, and national security.

Keyword(s): CBRNC; nuclear weapons of mass destruction; antiterrorism; nuclear terrorism; combating terrorism; counterterrorism


Pringle, Peter. "Terrorism: America's Newest Wargame," <u>Nation</u>, 267, No. 15, November 9, 1998, 11-15, 17.

The article examines how the threat of "catastrophic terrorism" is being used as a grand reorganization of the Pentagon, Central Intelligence Agency (CIA), and Federal Bureau of Investigation (FBI) bureaucracies to eliminate the perennial agency overlaps and gaps between "foreign" and "domestic" terrorism. The pace at which the threat has taken center stage as the prime threat to U.S. security is almost as unnerving as the threat itself. The article suggests that there is a tendency to hype the threat. By rushing to meet the new threat with new departments of counterespionage and counterweapons, there is a risk that the old art of deterrence through international treaties will take a back seat. The challenges of protecting Americans from a massive biological terrorist attack are examined.

Keyword(s): terrorism; CBRNC; biological weapons of mass destruction; combating terrorism; counterterrorism; antiterrorism


Rappe, Gene. "Should Insurers Cover Terrorism?," <u>National Underwriter: Property and Casualty/Risk and Benefits Management</u>, 103, No. 2, January 11, 1999, 7, 12.

In comparison with the cost of natural calamities, an act of terrorism could one day far surpass the loss costs paid out for a storm or a flood. At issue is whether insurers should modify their policies to include language that excludes damages arising out of terrorism. No simple answer exists today. One can argue a case for either position. To exclude damages arising out of a terrorist's act is an extremely anticonsumer position to take. If the damage caused by terrorists were excluded, at issue is whether such an exclusion should fall under war exclusions or should stand alone. Regardless, such a decision can only result in controversy. Insurers must carefully consider the fortuitous nature of the event, their customers' needs, and the effect that such an exclusion will have on the consumer at large.

Keyword(s): antiterrorism; combating terrorism; terrorism; CBRNC

Reid, E.O. "Evolution of a Body of Knowledge: An Analysis of Terrorism Research," Information Processing and Management, 33, No. 1, January 1997, 91-106.

This study provides an analysis of the development of contemporary terrorism research in the United States. Using on-line bibliometrics, tracing, and citation analysis, it explores how terrorism researchers interacted with other knowledge producers to shape the perception of terrorism. The results indicate that the research area was influenced directly by knowledge producers such as the media and the U.S. government. They had major impacts on the definitions of terrorism, the types of data used in analysis, and the diffusion of ideas. This resulted in the creation of invisible colleges of pro-Western terrorism researchers and a generation of many terrorism studies from a one-sided perspective of terrorism from below. [RH}

Keyword(s): terrorism; antiterrorism; combating terrorism


Resing, Dave. "A Line in the Sand: America's First Responders and the Use of Weapons of Mass Destruction," Police Chief, 65, No. 6, June 1998, 68-71.

The article assesses the increasing threat of terrorist use of a weapon of mass destruction against the general population of the United States and strategies by the emergency response infrastructure. It recommends and describes training and equipment for groups that will provide effective action under such conditions.

Keyword(s): CBRNC; first responders; chemical terrorism; nuclear terrorism; biological terrorism


Riley, Kevin Jack and Bruce Hoffman. Domestic Terrorism: A National Assessment of State and Local Preparedness. Santa Monica, California: Rand, 1995. [Call Number: HV6432.R55 1995]

The study reports on state and local preparedness in the U.S. for dealing with terrorist attacks of various types, as surveyed by the Rand Corporation. Included are statistics and evaluation of recent terrorist activity in the U.S. and a compilation of training and organizational conditions for state and local authorities.

Keyword(s): antiterrorism; terrorist groups and activities; first responders


Rittenhouse, Tod. "Designing Terrorist-Resistant Buildings," Fire Engineering, 148, November 1995, 103-5.

The Oklahoma City bombing has taught structural engineering an important lesson: Buildings must be designed to contend with the strains inflicted on them by a terrorist bomb. Designing terrorist-resistant features into buildings would have two main goals. The first objective would be to end up with buildings that will not fail when attacked. The second would be to design buildings in such a way that, in the event of an attack, rescue professionals would be able to gain quick access to the damaged building to tend to survivors. The most important improvement would be to improve the structure's ductility and incorporate some structural redundancy to prevent catastrophic failure or progressive collapse. When more than 80 percent of deaths are caused by the structure of the building falling on its occupants, it would be prudent for money to be spent on proper design and reinforcement. In addition, features such as limiting fenestration and using toughened glazing would reduce injuries caused by flying glass.

Keyword(s): technology; infrastructure protection; protecting structures; building collapse; building rescue and evacuation; antiterrorism; combating terrorism; blast mitigation

Roberts, Sandra. "Taggants Are No Match for Malicious Use of Explosives," Chemical Engineering, 105, No. 4, April 1998, 45.

A study by the National Research Council in Washington, D.C., released in March 1998, has concluded that additives used to tag explosives and trace their origin are not practical enough for broad use in the United States. According to the study, safety, cost, effectiveness, and environmental concerns must be addressed before a detection method can be mandated. The use of chemical markers is supported only for detection of plastic and sheet explosives, which pose a serious risk for airports because they can pass through metal detectors. The article discusses the issues involved.

Keyword(s): technology; terrorism; inspection of carry-on luggage; inspection of aircraft passengers; antiterrorism; combating terrorism; improvised explosive device threat or analysis; weapons technology

Rouhi, Maureen. "NRC Taking Another Look at Tagging Explosives," Chemical and Engineering News, 76, January 26, 1998, 11.

At the request of Congress, the National Research Council has set up a second committee to investigate the feasibility of tagging explosives to deter their illegal use. The new panel, which will only study issues related to smokeless and black powders, held an inaugural meeting on January 14-16, 1998, in Washington, D.C. The panel will review earlier efforts at tagging these powders and new technologies under development. In addition, it will investigate whether tagging would pose a risk to human life or safety, help law enforcement agents in their investigations, impair the quality and performance of the powders, have a negative influence on the environment, and so forth.

Keyword(s): technology; weapons technology; improvised explosive device threat or analysis; terrorism; combating terrorism; antiterrorism

Rouhi, Maureen. "Tagging Explosives: Safety and Cost Dominate Debate," Chemical and Engineering News, 75, January 20, 1997, 9-10.

The National Research Council committee organized to evaluate the value of tagging explosives as a counterterrorism measure held its first public hearing in January 1997 in Washington, D.C. The panel heard from industrial and special interest groups, firms with commercial or potential tagging technologies, and law enforcement agents. The breadth of interest in the hearings emphasizes the complexity of the committee's task.

Keyword(s): technology; weapons technology; improvised explosive device threat or analysis; terrorism; antiterrorism; combating terrorism; counterterrorism


Ruppe, David. "Cyberterrorism: Administration Reaches Out To Private Sector," White House Weekly, 19, No. 29, July 20, 1998, 1, 5.

Senior government officials told an American Bar Association conference in Washington, D.C., on July 15, 1998, that unprecedented public and private sector cooperation will be needed to defend against future cyberterrorism and other unconventional threats to critical U.S. infrastructure. A May 1998 Presidential Directive (PDD-63) orders the strengthening of U.S. defenses against emerging critical infrastructure (CI) threats. However, mistrust of the federal government and concerns about proprietary information could make cooperation challenging. The article discusses White House efforts to implement PDD-63 and its sister, PDD-62, which calls for a systematic, national approach to dealing with terrorism involving weapons of mass destruction.

Keyword(s): cyberterrorism; information assurance; CBRNC; counterterrorism; combating terrorism


Sadler, A.E., ed.. Urban Terrorism. San Diego: Greenhaven Press, 1996. [Call Number: HV6432.U73 1996]

The book is a collection of essays on four questions: Should Americans fear urban terrorism? Which groups pose an urban terrorist threat? Do the media encourage terrorism? and Do antiterrorism measures threaten civil liberties? Each question is answered in several different ways in the essays of the respective sections, with diametrically opposed views often juxtaposed. The authors are journalists, researchers, and academics.

Keyword(s): terrorism (general); terrorist groups and activities; antiterrorism


Schechter, Mitchell. "Security: 'It's Everyone's Job': Checking the History of Prospective Employees and Training Employees to Participate in Security Measures Are Among the Strategies Airline Caterers Are Using to Minimize the Threat of Terrorism," Food Management, 33, No. 1, 1998, 24-26.

Interviews with inflight food service and security experts provide insight on how inflight meal providers are preparing to defend their programs against the threat of terrorism. Dobbs International (Memphis, Tennessee) is expanding its security efforts beyond such Federal Aviation Administration mandates as compulsory background checks and verifications of work and personal histories. Dobbs now provides its employees with training and other means of preventing security breaches. The article mentions the other measures undertaken by inflight meal providers to prevent security breaches.

Keyword(s): terrorism; antiterrorism; combating terrorism

Schoenburg, Angus Von. "Problem Shooting," Airfinance Journal, No. 191, January 1997, 38-41.

Asset management may sound boring, but events such as the recent hostage situation on a Sudan Airways A310 in London show that the asset manager needs to be prepared for the unexpected. That particular case involved the British police, the bomb squad, and the aircraft managers, Fortis Aviation. Fortis manages the Sudan Airways A310 on behalf of a Belgian bank-led syndicate, which owns the aircraft. In this capacity, Fortis was able to provide the police with detailed plans of the aircraft's interior configuration and advise the bomb squad on where explosives could have been hidden aboard the aircraft. Asset management includes a number of distinct components. The fundamental elements relate to the commercial and technical management of existing aircraft leases. But many providers of these services also included the establishment of new lease contracts and remarketing in their portfolio of products.

Keyword(s): aviation security; inspection of aircraft cargo containers; combating terrorism; antiterrorism

Schwartz, Daniel M. "Environmental Terrorism: Analyzing the Concept," Journal of Peace Research, 35, No. 4, July 1998, 483-96.

Although the term "environmental terrorism" (or "ecological terrorism") is used in North American politics, media, and academia, the concept of environmental terrorism remains ambiguous. The author asks when is it appropriate to label environmental destruction "environmental terrorism"? He argues that the term has been misused by North American politicians, media, and academics. To remedy the semantic problem, he proposes a taxonomy that allows one to discern systematically the types of environmental destruction that can legitimately be labeled "terrorism" and those that can be called "environmental terrorism." He maintains that environmental destruction or the threat thereof can be labeled "terrorism" when: (1) the act or threat breaches national and/or international laws governing the disruption of the environment during peacetime or wartime; and (2) the act or threat exhibits the fundamental characteristics of terrorism (i.e., the act or threat of violence has specific objectives, and the violence is aimed at a symbolic target). He concludes that an act of environmental destruction can be termed "environmental terrorism" only when the two latter criteria are met, and when the environment is used by the perpetrator as an authentic symbol that instills fear in the larger population over the ecological consequences of the act.

Keyword(s): terrorism (general); terrorist groups and activities; combating terrorism

Scott, David. "Facing Our Worst Nightmare," NFPA Journal, 91, May-June 1997, 52-6.

As the threat of terrorism increases throughout the United States, the fire service is preparing for future attacks. Funding for fire service training and equipment has been raised, and the emerging level of interagency cooperation is unprecedented. The fire service and other emergency responders must adopt the principles of alertness and preparedness in order to meet the challenges posed by terrorists.

Keyword(s): antiterrorism; combating terrorism; building rescue and evacuation; first responders

Scott, David. "It Could Happen Here," NFPA Journal, 92, January-February 1998, 38-43.

Emergency personnel in several U.S. cities have experienced a new kind of terrorist response training. The terrorism preparedness programs are designed to help communities recognize and tap the state and federal resources available. The terrorist response training discussed uses a case study of an attack on Quincy Market in Boston, Massachusetts.

Keyword(s): antiterrorism; combating terrorism; biological terrorism; chemical terrorism; CBRNC; biological weapons of mass destruction; chemical weapons of mass destruction; nuclear terrorism

Scott, William B. "Noninvasive Detector Identifies Chemical Weapon Agents," Aviation Week and Space Technology, 148, No. 20, May 18, 1998, 69-70.

A new system for noninvasively detecting chemical agents in air-delivered weapons could deflate protests that disarmament inspectors are engaging in industrial espionage and compromising the secrets of a nation's pharmaceutical and chemical industries. It also will speed up monitoring processes, improve the reliability of findings, and protect inspectors from deadly nerve agents. A ruggedized prototype of the handheld system is being field-tested on various munitions by the United States Defense Special Weapons Agency, one of the project's sponsors.

Keyword(s): antiterrorism; combating terrorism; CBRNC; chemical weapons of mass destruction; technology; counterterrorism

Seiple, Chris. "Consequence Management: Domestic Response to Weapons of Mass Destruction," Parameters, 27, No. 3, Autumn 1997, 119-34.

Taking as a given that weapons of mass destruction (CBRNC) will be used against the United States by terrorists, the author discusses how the United States is prepared to manage the consequences of such an incident. After discussing definitions and terms of reference, the article focuses on the Chemical-Biological Incident Response Force and the 1996 Summer Olympics. The article concludes with a discussion of continuing issues and recommendations.

Keyword(s): CBRNC; chemical weapons of mass destruction; biological weapons of mass destruction; antiterrorism; combating terrorism; counterterrorism; first responders

Selden, Zachary. Assessing the Biological Weapons Threat. Washington: Business Executives for National Security, 1997.

The report assesses the threat that biological weapons will be used by rogue states or terrorist organizations, which in the author's view is quite a likely prospect. He proposes a three-pronged strategy of transparency, detection, and defense, the first step of which depends on substantial increases in international cooperation (e.g., the Biological Weapons Convention).

Keyword(s): biological terrorism; future trends

Serrano, Richard A. <u>One of Ours</u>. New York and London: W.W. Norton, 1998. [Call Number: HV6432.S47 1998]

The book is a psychological study of Timothy McVeigh, the Oklahoma City bomber. It traces the development of the views that led to the crime, as well as the methodology and strategy that formed the crime itself. The account offers much biographical detail and eyewitness accounts, with no direct analysis of the bombing as a terrorist act.

Keyword(s): terrorism (general); terrorist groups and activities

Shanahan, Ed. "Doomsday Dept. (New York City's Office of Emergency Management)," <u>New York</u>, 31, March 16, 1998, 30.

The Office of Emergency Management is now responsible for managing disaster-relief in New York, including chemical or biological attacks. In November 1997, a four-hour drill on Greenwich Street in TriBeCa, the biggest and most visible event of its kind in the city, showed what New York is capable of dealing with. It was the latest of a dozen similar exercises conducted over the past few years.

Keyword(s): first responders; antiterrorism; combating terrorism

Shifrin, Carole A. "Airports on Track in Deploying New-Technology Security," <u>Aviation Week and Space Technology</u>, 149, No. 10, September 7, 1998, 166-69.

U.S. airports are installing the latest-technology aviation security equipment, including explosive detection systems and automated X-ray machines for screening checked and carry-on baggage. Installation has been stepped up as a result of the heightened security alert following U.S. military strikes against suspected terrorist facilities in Afghanistan and Sudan.

Keyword(s): technology; aviation security; inspection of aircraft cargo containers; inspection of carry-on luggage; inspection of aircraft passengers; antiterrorism; combating terrorism

Shubik, Martin. "Terrorism, Technology, and the Socioeconomics of Death," <u>Comparative Strategy: An International Journal</u>, [London], 16:4, 1997, 399-414.

Contending that warfare is facing a paradigmatic shift, the author notes that the increasingly cheap availability of technical information and dual-use material is making mass killing possible for small groups, or even for individuals. Biological weapons, with their easy accessibility, lack of effective international controls, and disproportionately great effectiveness, offer a singularly attractive mix to radical groups. Because of what he sees as the inevitable use of biological weapons by terrorists, the author argues that the United States must radically rethink how it hopes to deal with biological warfare initiated by terrorists and fringe groups, given the likely ineffectiveness of current policies.

Keyword(s): technology; biological terrorism; biological weapons of mass destruction; counterterrorism; combating terrorism; CBRNC; terrorism

Simon, J. D. "Biological Terrorism: Preparing to Meet the Threat," Journal of the American Medical Association, 278, No. 5, August 1997, 428-430.

The threat of terrorists using biological warfare agents has received increased attention in recent years. Despite the hope that--with the right combination of policies, security measures, and intelligence gathering--a major biological warfare terrorist attack can be prevented, the history of conventional terrorism indicates otherwise. Biological terrorism can best be combated by focusing on how best to respond to a terrorist attack. The medical and emergency service communities will play the most important role in that process. Ensuring that they are trained to recognize the symptoms of diseases caused by biological warfare agents and have Critical Incident Stress Debriefing teams available to help them cope with the emotional aspects of treating exposed survivors should be part of contingency planning. By improving U.S. readiness to respond to biological terrorism, many lives can be saved, and terrorists can be denied their goal of creating panic and crisis throughout the country.

Keyword(s): CBRNC; biological weapons of mass destruction; biological terrorism; biological agent detection; first responders; combating terrorism; antiterrorism

Siuru, Bill, and Andrea Stewart. "New Technologies for Finding Felons, Terrorists, and Evidence," Electronics Now, 69, No. 4, April 1998, 13-15.

Unique electronic technologies being developed for law enforcement have applications for detecting bombs as well as terrorists. The Enclosed Space Detection System (ESDS), developed by the Department of Energy's Oak Ridge National Laboratory (ORNL) and Lockheed Martin Energy Systems, Inc., can "hear" the heartbeat of someone hiding in a car or a truck. A new explosives-detection system being developed by the Sandia National Laboratory could greatly reduce the threat of terrorists carrying explosives into an airport or other public building. In the evidence-detection portal, a "puff" of air is blown over a person, and an air sample is collected and analyzed by a spectrometer. Sandia's new evidence detector makes fingerprints and other organic material actually blink when special glasses are worn, so that crime-scene investigators can locate potential evidence quickly.

Keyword(s): technology; antiterrorism; combating terrorism; automatic portal inspection; fingerprint analysis/recovery; inspection of overseas containers; inspecting vehicles automatically; inspection of aircraft cargo containers; inspection of aircraft cargo containers; biological agent detection; inspection of carry-on luggage; inspection of aircraft passengers; vehicle inspection

Sloan, Stephen. Terrorism: National Security Policy and the Home Front. Carlisle Barracks, Pennsylvania: U.S. Army War College, 1995. [Call Number: HV6431.T483 1995]

The chapter identifies changes in the international climate and the resulting new threats of terrorist activity in the United States. It then describes technological and operational changes that can be expected by those conducting such activity, followed by an assessment of potential terrorist targets and operational approaches.

Keyword(s): antiterrorism; nuclear terrorism; biological terrorism

Smith, Brent L., and Kelly R. Damphousse. "Two Decades of Terror: Characteristics, Trends, and Prospects for the Future of American
Terrorism." Pages 132-154 in The Future of Terrorism: Violence in the New Millennium. Harvey W. Kushner, ed. Thousand Oaks, CA: Sage Publications, 1998. [Call Number: HV6432.F87 1998]

This chapter presents data on domestic U.S. terrorism since 1980 based on court records of federally indicted domestic terrorists. It reviews changes in the patterns, characteristics, and tactics of U.S. terrorists and of federal investigative and prosecutorial strategies; it also looks at the near future of terrorism in the U.S. The focus is on the emergence of right-wing terrorist groups and on patterns of federal prosecution in dealing with terrorism. The authors find that right-wing, antifederal violence is the greatest threat for the immediate future in contrast with left-wing violence in the 1960s and 1970s.

Keyword(s): combating terrorism; future trends; terrorist groups and activities; terrorism

Soenmez, Sevil F., and Alan R. Graefe. "Influence of Terrorism Risk on Foreign Tourism Decisions," Annals of Tourism Research, 25, No. 1, January 1998, 112-44.

The article examines eight independent variables: international travel experience, risk-perception level, travel attitude, age, gender, education, income, and presence of children in a household. The study is based on a mail survey of 240 tourists from the United States, Puerto Rico, and the U.S. Virgin Islands, conducted during the spring of 1994. It reviews bombing and other terrorist attacks involving tourists, during the 1972-96 period.

Keyword(s): terrorism; terrorist groups and activities; combating terrorism; antiterrorism

Stambaugh, Hollis, Chris Tillery, and Philip Schaenman. "Inventory of State and Local Law Enforcement Technology Needs to Combat Terrorism," Research in Brief: National Institute of Justice, January 1999, 1-6.

To fulfill its congressional tasking to determine what technologies are needed by state and local law enforcement agencies to combat terrorism, the National Institute of Justice (NIJ) inventoried the technology needs of state and local law enforcement, with respondents from all 50 states and the District of Columbia. The technology needs expressed were remarkably similar across the country. Affordability appears to be an overarching concern of state and local law enforcement agencies. They are often not as well equipped as the terrorists they may face. State and local law enforcement are particularly concerned about their ability to handle nuclear, biological, and chemical (NBC) devices and other weapons of mass destruction. Another concern is that state and local law enforcement generally lack the ability to combat cyberterrorism effectively. They realize that it requires cooperation among federal, state, and local law enforcement agencies as well as cooperation between law enforcement and other agencies.

Keyword(s): technology; combating terrorism; antiterrorism; counterterrorism

Stephenson, J. "Confronting a Biological Armageddon: Experts Tackle Prospect of Bioterrorism," JAMA [Journal of the American Medical Association], 276, No. 5, August 7, 1996, 349-51.

Government and military officials believe that the possibility of a terrorist strike that involves infectious agents such as viruses is greater in 1996 than at any time in the past. Numerous multiagency task forces are stepping up their training to ensure that they can adequately protect the public.

Keyword(s): biological terrorism; CBRNC; antiterrorism; combating terrorism; first responders; biological weapons of mass destruction

Stube, Peter M. "Incidents Involving Weapons of Mass Destruction," Fire Engineering, 151, No. 11, November 1998, 38, 40, 42.

Since the sarin nerve agent attack in the Tokyo subway system in 1995, emergency services in the United States have undergone a transformation. Response protocols have been improved and updated, and new protocols have been put into place throughout the fire service. A great nationwide effort is being made to train personnel to respond to incidents involving weapons of mass destruction (CBRNC). The article discusses the problems associated with detecting incidents of chemical-biological (CB) terrorism. It notes that no good detection devices are available for use in warning of a release or in quickly identifying a biologic agent in the field. A chemical incident requires an immediate and active role, whereas a biological incident requires accurate diagnosis and timely treatment by the medical community.

Keyword(s): biological weapons of mass destruction; chemical weapons of mass destruction; technology; CBRNC; first responders; antiterrorism; combating terrorism

Szyliowicz, Joseph, and Paul Viotti. "Dilemmas of Transportation Security," Transportation Quarterly, 51, Spring 1997, 79-95.

This article discusses social factors, bureaucracy, the role of U.S. intelligence, the structure of U.S. security, and the global context. There is some focus on aviation, efforts by the Federal Aviation Administration (FAA), and other organizations to combat terrorism.

Keyword(s): aviation; terrorism; antiterrorism; combating terrorism

Tarlach, Gemma M. "The Threat of Biochemical Attacks Offers Role for R. Ph.s," Drug Topics, 142, No. 6, March 16, 1998, 46.

The federal government recently began a multimillion-dollar effort to prepare for the possibility of a domestic biochemical attack. Such an event, experts say, would put hospital pharmacists on the front line. Metropolitan Medical Strike Teams will provide the crucial initial response to an attack, including patient and site decontamination and the supply of antibiotics, antidotes, and vaccines.

Keyword(s): CBRNC; chemical weapons of mass destruction; first responders; antiterrorism; combating terrorism; biological weapons of mass destruction


Tenet, George J. "Cyber War Threat Is Real and Growing," Aviation Week and Space Technology, 148, No. 17, April 27, 1998, 78.

This article consists of excerpts from "Information Security Risks, Opportunities, and the Bottom Line," an address delivered by the U.S. director of Central Intelligence at a NationsBank Policy Forum held at the Georgia Institute of Technology in Atlanta. The writer discusses the real and increasing danger to U.S. information systems from foreign entities. The number of known potential adversaries conducting research on information attacks is increasing rapidly and includes intelligence services, military organizations, terrorists, criminals, industrial competitors, hackers, and aggrieved or disloyal insiders. Foreign governments and their military services are paying increased attention to the concept of information warfare. The United States needs to develop a totally new way of thinking about this problem. What is needed is obvious to all--security. What is less discussed is the need to bind a system of trust to the security systems. The need for cooperation between government and industry in building trustworthy key management infrastructure is paramount to meeting our common interests of networks that meet business needs without introducing vulnerability in those systems.

Keyword(s): technology; cyberterrorism; information warfare; combating terrorism; antiterrorism


Tomajczyk, Stephen F. U.S. Elite Counter-Terrorist Forces. Osceola, Wisconsin: Motorbooks, 1997. [Call Number: HV6432.T65 1997]

The book gives a wide-ranging background on terrorist activity in the United States and responses and responding organizations, including descriptions and histories of various military and civilian forces designated for antiterrorist and first-response activities. Also included are listings and descriptions of training and equipment used by such groups.

Keyword(s): counterterrorism; antiterrorism; first responders


Tucker, David. "Responding to Terrorism," The Washington Quarterly, 21, No. 1, Winter 1998, 103-17.

As attacks on Americans and the attention paid them have increased, officials have reportedly conducted the same debates about how to respond to terrorism that their predecessors had ten years earlier, when terrorism was at a high point. The article examines the relative merits of the U.S. "no concessions" policy, prosecution as the principal response to terrorist acts committed in the United States, the use of economic sanctions, the use of military force, negotiating treaties and conventions, addressing terrorism's causes, defending against terrorism, preempting terrorism, and disrupting terrorists. The author concludes that success has come when the United States has combined all of these options and taken advantage of circumstances. Thus, additional ways to combine these methods need to be found.

Keyword(s): combating terrorism; counterterrorism; antiterrorism; terrorism (general)

Tucker, Phebe, Betty Pfefferbaum, Robert Vincent, Sharron D. Boehler, and Sara Jo Nixon. "Oklahoma City: Disaster Challenges Mental Health and Medical Administrators," Journal of Behavioral Health Sciences and Research, 25, No. 1, February 1998, 93-99.

Mental health and medical administrators responded to the Oklahoma City bombing in April 1996 with cooperative and overlapping efforts to meet community needs in the wake of terrorism. The major agencies assisted in the immediate rescue response, organized crisis hotlines, prepared mental health professionals to counsel bereaved families and victims, organized debriefing of rescuers, assessed mental health needs of local school children, planned for longer-term treatment, and coordinated research efforts to learn from the disaster. The article also discusses implications to mental health administrators responding to significant acts of terrorism.

Keyword(s): first responders; antiterrorism; counterterrorism; combating terrorism

United States Federal Bureau of Investigation. Terrorist Research and Analytical Center. National Security Division. Terrorism in the United States 1995. Washington, D.C.: United States Department of Justice, 1995. [Call Number: BV6432.T46 1995]

This annual report describes the year's major terrorist acts and the apprehension of suspects in those cases. It includes a short section on current trends in terrorism in the United States, including the use of unconventional weapons. Accounts include the methodology used by terrorists and by the FBI in apprehension and prevention activities. There is no record of more recent issues of this annual.

Keyword(s): terrorism; chemical terrorism; biological terrorism

United States General Accounting Office. Aviation Security: Implementation of Recommendations is Under Way, but Completion Will Take Several Years. Washington, D.C.: GAO, 1998. [Call Number: TL725.3.S44 U54 1998]

The report details the Federal Aviation Administration's steps to comply with the 5-step recommendations of the White House Committee on Aviation Safety and Security to improve airport security in the United States. It provides a step-by-step account of the government procedures taken to achieve the goals and the various obstacles encountered on the way. Included is a detailed listing of equipment, systems, and methodologies deployed and planned for deployment.

Keyword(s): inspection of aircraft carry-on luggage; inspection of aircraft passengers; inspection of aircraft cargo containers

United States General Accounting Office. Combating Terrorism: Threat and Risk Assessments Can Help Prioritize and Target Program Investments. Washington, D.C.: GAO, 1998.

The pamphlet describes the formation and goals of the 1996 Nunn-Lugar-Domenici (NLD) domestic preparedness program, aimed at aiding U.S. cities in responding to potential terrorist attacks using weapons of mass destruction. Discussed are the threat- and risk-assessment techniques of private entities that were investigated and the elements that could be adopted in the NLD program. The concept of such assessments also is described as it fits with the requirements of national antiterrorism security programs.

Keyword(s): antiterrorism; first responders; CBRNC

United States. Congress. 104th, 2d Session. House. Committee on Transportation and Infrastructure. Subcommittee on Aviation. Aviation Security and Anti-Terrorism Efforts: Hearing, September 11, 1996. Washington, D.C.: GPO, Superintendent of Documents, 1997.

The hearing reviews the state of aviation security in the United States, whether it needs to be upgraded, the impact on the cost and efficiency of the national system in light of the crash of TWA Flight 800, and the threat of sophisticated domestic and international terrorism.

Keyword(s): aviation security; antiterrorism; counterterrorism

United States. Congress. 104th. 2d Session. House. Select Committee on Intelligence. Terrorism--Looking Ahead: Issues and Options for Congress; Proceedings of a Seminar Held by the Congressional Research Service December 7, 1995. Washington, D.C.: GPO, 1996. [Call Number: HV6432.T464 1996]

The records of this seminar provide expert testimony on the current level and nature of terrorist threats to the U.S. from individuals in the intelligence community. Discussion included law enforcement preventive measures, new trends in terrorist threats including biological terrorism, intelligence collection methods, and the nature of counterterrorism.

Keyword(s): terrorism; biological terrorism; antiterrorism; counterterrorism; terrorist groups and activities

United States. Congress. 105th, 1st Session. House. Committee on National Security. Subcommittee on Military Research and Development. The Federal Response to Domestic Terrorism Involving Weapons of Mass Destruction and the Status of the Department of Defense Support Program. Washington, D.C.: GPO, Superintendent of Documents, 1998.

These hearings, held on November 4, 1997, examine the federal response to domestic terrorism involving weapons of mass destruction and the status of the Department of Defense Support Program.

Keyword(s): CBRNC; chemical terrorism; counterterrorism; biological terrorism; combating terrorism; antiterrorism


United States. Congress. 105th, 1st Session. Senate. Committee on the Judiciary. Subcommittee on Technology, Terrorism, and Government Information. The Encryption Debate: Criminals, Terrorists, and the Security Needs of Business and Industry: Hearing, September 3, 1997. Washington, D.C.: GPO, Superintendent of Documents, 1998.

This Senate Judiciary Committee hearing, held on September 3, 1997, consists of testimony from the Federal Bureau of Investigation (FBI), a panel of academic experts, and a panel of industry experts. It is concerned with the impact of encryption technology on public safety and law enforcement. It focuses on the security needs of business and industry and the use of encryption by organized crime and terrorists.

Keyword(s): cyberterrorism; information assurance; combating terrorism; antiterrorism


United States. Congress. Senate. Joint Hearing Before the Senate Judiciary Subcommittee on Technology, Terrorism, and Government Information and the Senate Select Committee on Intelligence. Chemical and Biological Weapons Threats to America: Are We Prepared?. Washington, D.C.: GPO, Superintendent of Documents, April 22, 1998.

This is a hearing on the recent efforts to create a national strategy to prevent and respond to a terrorist attack involving chemical and biological weapons (CBW). Testimony is delivered from Attorney General Janet Reno and Federal Bureau of Investigation (FBI) Director Louis Freeh on federal response plans. There is also discussion of the former Soviet Union's biological weapons program and the Iraqi gassing of Halabja.

Keyword(s): CBRNC; biological weapons of mass destruction; biological terrorism; combating terrorism; antiterrorism; future trends


United States. Congress. Senate. Testimony Before the U.S. Senate Committee on Armed Services. Worldwide Threats Facing the United States. Washington, D.C.: GPO, Superintendent of Documents, February 6, 1997.

A Pentagon official, Lieutenant General Patrick M. Hughes, and the director of the Central Intelligence Agency (CIA), George J. Tenet, provide testimony addressing many different threats posed to the United

States. They specifically discuss the threat of chemical and biological (CB) terrorism and the proliferation of chemical and biological warfare (CBW) technology.

Keyword(s): CBRNC; chemical weapons of mass destruction; chemical terrorism; biological terrorism; future trends; combating terrorism; antiterrorism; biological weapons of mass destruction

United States. Department of Health and Human Services. Seminar on Responding to the Consequences of Chemical and Biological Terrorism. Washington, D.C.: GPO, 1997.

The seminar report discusses the requirements for health and medical services personnel and organizations responding to biological and chemical terrorist acts, in the context of national defense policy. A central theme is effective allocation of limited resources and optimally effective administrative structures and procedures.

Keyword(s): first responders; chemical terrorism; biological terrorism

United States. General Accounting Office. Combating Terrorism: Status of DOD Efforts to Protect Its Forces Overseas. Washington, D.C.: GAO, 1997.

The report summarizes the findings of the Downing task forces, assigned after the Khobar (Saudi Arabia) bombing of 1996 to recommend improvements in U.S. troop security in high-risk countries. Included are the steps DOD had taken at that point to improve security and a list of recommendations for further improvements, including vulnerability assessment, standardization of physical security and security countermeasures throughout the Armed Forces, and clarified individual responsibilities. Special emphasis is placed on Turkey and Saudi Arabia.

Keyword(s): antiterrorism; intelligence; future trends

United States. General Accounting Office. Terrorism and Drug Trafficking: Threats and Roles of Explosives and Narcotics Detection Technology. Washington, D.C.: GAO, 1996. [Call Number: HV6432.T445 1996]

The report to Congress outlines threats of terrorist attacks on civilian aviation, existing strategies to meet those threats, and future strategies and technologies. Included are evaluations of the effectiveness of current equipment and methods and an assessment of threat posed by various vectors, as well as estimates of cost and effectiveness of some projected security systems.

Keyword(s): inspection of overseas containers; aviation; antiterrorism

Vegar, Jose. "Terrorism's New Breed: Threat of Chemical and Biological Weapons," <u>Bulletin of the Atomic Scientists</u>, 54, March-April 1998, 50-55.

The new breed of terrorists might be more likely to employ chemical or biological weapons than conventional ones. Recent attacks in America fit a well-known pattern for terrorist activity: The attacks were not aimed at a particular person but instead at a random number of people, and all intended to use conventional weapons. Many in the antiterrorist community are unsure how much longer such attacks will be the rule, however, and wonder whether terrorists will start to strike at larger numbers of people--for political, religious, ethnic, or racial reasons--via the use of weapons of mass destruction. Eradicating a threat that is highly dispersed, diffused, complicated, and largely posed by clandestine organizations is very difficult, and most analysts believe the majority of antiterrorism resources ought to be given over to intelligence-gathering and law-enforcement agencies.

Keyword(s): CBRNC; chemical weapons of mass destruction; biological weapons of mass destruction; biological terrorism; antiterrorism; combating terrorism; counterterrorism; chemical terrorism

Venzke, Ben N. <u>First Responder Chem-Bio Handbook: Practical</u> <u>Manual for First Responders</u>. Alexandria, Virginia: Tempest Publishers, 1998.

This small-format handbook (6.5 x 5, spiral bound) was designed as an easy-to-carry reference guide for police, fire, security, and emergency medical service (EMS) personnel who may be in a position to respond to an incident involving chemical and/or biological warfare agents. It discusses initial assessment, signs and symptoms, diagnosis, treatment, decontamination, and precautions. There is also a section devoted to the establishment of a decontaminization zone. The book provides all the key information needed during the first few critical moments of an incident.

Keyword(s): first responders; antiterrorism; counterterrorism; combating terrorism

Wehde, Ed. "Cyberterrorism Red Alert," <u>Communications</u> <u>International</u>, 24, No. 12, December 1997, 34.

Increasing reliance on computers and the Internet, combined with ever-increasing interconnectivity, creates enormous potential for people to commit crimes and create disorder via the Internet. Critical infrastructures, such as water treatment plants, power systems, and transportation controls, are the most likely targets. The President's Commission on Critical Infrastructure Protection makes several recommendations to alleviate the threat, including a public education program, a best-practices policy to protect against cyberterrorism, keeping laws in step with technology, and more research and development.

Keyword(s): cyberterrorism; infrastructure protection; antiterrorism; combating terrorism

Welsh, Edward J. "Federal Laboratory, Agency Team for Counterterrorism Initiative," <u>Signal</u>, 53, No. 4, December 1998, VG7.

The Federal Bureau of Investigation (FBI) is adopting high-technology research weapons in an effort to find suspected terrorists and combat terrorist attacks against citizens and government facilities. The FBI will collaborate with the Lawrence Livermore National Laboratory in counterterrorism efforts.

Keyword(s): antiterrorism; combating terrorism; technology; counterterrorism


Wiant, Chris J. "Biological Weapons: What Role Should Environmental Health Specialists Take in Protecting Our Communities?," Journal of Environmental Health, 60, No. 9, May 1998, 25, 65.

Although biological weapons present a threat when used on the battlefield, the greatest risk might be delivery of such pathogens through terrorist acts. The author describes the role that environmental health specialists should take in protecting U.S. communities.
Keyword(s): biological terrorism; CBRNC; antiterrorism; combating terrorism; biological weapons of mass destruction Williams, Alex. "Germ Warfear," New York, 31, No. 44, November 16, 1998, 28. The article contends that the next great urban anxiety is chemical and biological terrorism. It reports that New York City is strengthening its antiterrorism security and stockpiling vaccines, and that the Federal Bureau of Investigation (FBI) is running drills. The article also addresses what individual residents should be doing.

Keyword(s): CBRNC; chemical weapons of mass destruction; biological weapons of mass destruction; antiterrorism; combating terrorism


Winston, Paul D., and Kathryn J. McIntyre. "Germ Scare Shows Need for Preparation," Business Insurance, 32, No. 8, February 23, 1998, 25.

U.S. military forces and their allies have to be in a state of preparedness for war. Similarly, risk managers have to prepare for the worst and hope for the best when it comes to protecting their organizations from terrorism. The article discusses risk management as it relates to terrorism.

Keyword(s): terrorism; antiterrorism; combating terrorism


Zalud, B. "Focus on Government Facilities," Security, 35, No. 4, April 1998, 28-9.

From city hall to the Pentagon, officials are hardening their security to restrict access, monitor activity, and reduce the incidents of theft, violence, and terrorism. In a national study of security plans and procedures at federal, state, municipal, and correctional facilities, Security magazine has found that more security executives see agency regulations as more effective than building codes to provide a safe and secure environment. [RH}

Keyword(s): antiterrorism; combating terrorism; surveillance

Zeigler, James P. "The Dangers of Chemical Weapons," Occupational Health and Safety, 65, October 1996, 182-84.

The article examines training, planning, and protective equipment programs to enable civilian teams to respond to terrorist attacks or accidental release of toxic chemical warfare agents. The focus is on measures to cope with mass terrorism casualties in the United States. Emergency-response teams are struggling to prepare for casualties and exposure that they might face because of terrorism or an emergency release.

Keyword(s): CBRNC; chemical terrorism; biological terrorism


Zesiger, Sue. "Freeze!," Fortune, 135, No. 8, April 28, 1997, 417-20.
Gerry Smith of International Training, Inc. (ITI) is a former special agent with the Air Force Office of Special Investigations (OSI). When a terrorist makes a successful attack, Smith gets called in as a post-incident consultant to determine what happened and what went wrong. In his day job, he teaches 5,000 students each year how to frustrate would-be assassins. Many of the company's clients are corporate executives and so-called high-wealth individuals. Smith and his partner, Jerome Hoffman, also a former Air Force OSI agent, have been running these courses since 1989. The article focuses on ITI's antiterrorist evasive-driving course.

Keyword(s): antiterrorism; combating terrorism; counterterrorism